A REFRESHER COURSE

A STEP-BY-STEP PROGRAM TO INCREASED EMUNAH

A REFRESHER COURSE

A STEP-BY-STEP PROGRAM TO INCREASED EMUNAH

BY RABBI DOVID SAPIRMAN

Mosaica Press, Inc.

© 2015 by Mosaica Press

Edited by Doron Kornbluth

Typeset by Daniella Kirsch

All rights reserved

ISBN-10: 1-937887-55-3   ISBN-13: 978-1-937887-55-1

No part of this publication may be translated, reproduced, stored in a retrieval system or transmitted in any form or by any means, electronic, mechanical, photocopying, recording, or otherwise, without prior permission in writing from both the copyright holder and the publisher.

Published and distributed by:

Mosaica Press, Inc.

www.mosaicapress.com

info@mosaicapress.com

COPYRIGHT by ANI MAAMIN FOUNDATION

info@animaamin.org   845-418-2122

This volume and series

is dedicated in memory of

our parents

Joseph & Martha

Melohn ע״ה

ר׳ יוסף בן ר׳ אריה לייב הכהן ז״ל

נפטר כ׳ סיון תשמ״ג

ורעיתו מלכה פערל בת ר׳ מאיר ע״ה

נפטרה כ״ט ניסן תשע״ג

תנצב״ה

Leon and Simi Melohn

בס"ד

שמואל קמנצקי
Rabbi S. Kamenetsky

2018 Upland Way
Philadelphia, PA 19131

Home: 215-473-2798
Study: 215-473-1212

יום ששי לס' וירא

לכבוד ידידי אהובי הרה"ח ר' דוב סלומון
שליט"א

קבל נא את שבח וחומד להכפיס שאותי
עניני אמונה, בטוח אני שהחיזוק וגדולת אלוה
של אלוקי מדינן יעורר הרבה לא חשיבה.
כל מי שיאמין בהכרעת הפסוקים של שקר
כי זהו אמת רצון ד' בכחו יוכל לקיים מה
שאתה מבקשה יעזור דעל הבורה ויוכל לוין חיים
וראשונות של מתוקים.

ראתנים לך הרבים הטובים שעשו לכלל ישראל
הנדפסים ואת'"ה נזכה לגואל ד' בב' במהרה בימינו
אמן

ברכה רב חו"ש והצלחה
נאמן להרי'

שמואל קמנצקי

הרב אהרן פלדמן
RABBI AHARON FELDMAN
421 YESHIVA LANE, APT 3A, BALTIMORE, MD 21208
TEL: 410-6539433 FAX: 410-6534694
STUDY: 410-4847200 EXT. 114
E-MAIL: RAF@NIRC.EDU

ROSH HAYESHIVA
NER ISRAEL RABBINICAL COLLEGE

ראש הישיבה
ישיבת נר ישראל

בס"ד יב אייר תשע"ה

HASKAMA

Faced with virtually an entire Western world which does not subscribe to the beliefs of Jews regarding Creation and Mattan Torah, many of our youth need to be shown why they should accept these beliefs. Although the infinite wisdom of the world and of the Torah are in themselves the greatest evidence of their infinite Author, young people often need organized proofs to demonstrate this truth.

Rabbi Dovid Sapirman and his Ani Maamin Foundation have risen to the occasion and for many years have been demonstrating to the public, especially to the young public, that Jews believe in Torah not out of blind faith but because of irrefutable, logical reasoning. In this he follows in the footsteps of Rabbeynu Yehuda Halevy in his HaKuzari and others who have written on this topic.

Rabbi Sapirman has now organized his lectures into book form. I have no doubt that this book will be highly effective in bringing the Jewish public to a deeper belief and commitment to Torah and Mitzvos and am pleased to endorse it.

May this book hasten the time when the blessing of the Navi, "*Ve-eyrastich li be-emuna*"—"And I will wed you because of [your] faith," will be realized.

With blessings of the Torah,

Rabbi Aharon Feldman

בית המדרש - זכרון משה
ע"ש הר' משה יוסף בן שמעיהו ז"ל רייכמאנן

Rosh HaKollel
Rabbi Yaakov Hirschman

Rosh HaKollel
Rabbi Shlomo Miller

בס"ד

שלמה אליהו מילר
רה"כ ואב"ד דכולל טאראנטא

כ' סיון תשע"ה

הנה ידידי הנחמד הרב דוד סאפירמאן שליט"א רחש לבו דבר בראותו גודל רוח אפיקורסות בדורנו, וממילא רוח הטומאה הזאת חדר גם לתוך מחנה המאמינים. ובפרט לנערים ונערות אשר קבלתם בעקרי האמונה הוא מאבותם ויש הרבה שאין אמונתם שלמה בזה ובחדרי לבם לפעמים עולה ספק איך אני יודע שמה שלמדנו אבותי ורבותי הוא האמת לאמתו והספקות באים מכח רוח הטומאה והאפיקורסות השורה בחוצות. ע"כ יסד ידידי הנ"ל מוסד "אני מאמין" אשר המטרה שלו להחזיק האמונה בי"ג עיקרי האמונה ולהחזיק האמונה שתהא בבחינת אמונה שלמה שהיא ידיעה ברורה בלי שום מקום ספק.

ע"כ באתי בזה לעודדו ולהחזיקו ובטח שספרו יועיל להקוראים בו להחזיק יסוד האמונה אצלם. ואני מברכו שחפץ ד' בידו יצליח.

ובזכות האמונה נזכה בביאת המשיח ובנין בהמ"ק במהרה בימינו.

מרכז אגודת ישראל בטורונטו
AGUDATH ISRAEL CONGREGATION OF TORONTO
129 McGILLIVRAY AVE., TORONTO, ONTARIO, CANADA M5M 2Y7

בס"ד

RABBI:
MOSHE MORDECHAI LOWY

מרדכי לאווי שליט"א

חודש אדר שבועים הם לטוב
על שמחה בתהרת הפסוק
בי אתה עמדי פה העלה

על ידי ה.ה. המעולה איש אשכולות חונן
דעת ח"ו ישרים וגודל הסמי הגהיד לעשירן ה"י
"בית" הנאמן יחי"

הרב הגדול כ' בית סיני בתולת"ה הכל בו
ומעט לקטן ב' ל' עשרה לעמדו חן להשיב
את הנשיב ודת בכתב "וגדע ענת ואחוב
אובינן כי הם הולקים פאר שמע ותל
חידוש אמת ו' לעד יוכל לקיים את ה' אמן גידול
ביראה ח' ב' ה' לעשות גבהות אדירם ל' אפסי ארץ
וחיו חסין בטוב ה' וכי את ה' אחיו בדעתות

הנני מקדים לו שופע ענינו חיים ונחת
ברכת לגדול ה' ועוסק
מאת אבל לובי

Rosh HaKollel
Rabbi Yaakov Hirschman

בית המדרש - זכרון משה
ע"ש הר' משה יוסף בן שמעיהו ז"ל רייכמאנן

Rosh HaKollel
Rabbi Shlomo Miller

בס"ד

יעקב מיכאל הירשמן
רה"כ

כ"ב אייר תשע"ה

APPROBATION/הסכמה

The concept of מצות אנשים מלומדה, fulfilling מצות by rote - out of habit, without כונה intent and focus has already been eschewed by the נביא ישעיהו. The observance of מצות has to be done with awareness and thought.

The same certainly is true of אמונה and בטחון in the רבש"ע, and the immutable י"ג עיקרים the cornerstone of Torah True Judaism. The whole תורה was divinely given and the רבש"ע concurrently revealed to משה רבנו the oral Torah תורה שבעל פה. Although all believing Jews subscribe to these principles of the faith, much of it can be classified as מצות אנשים מלומדה.

We believe, because we are Jews and Jews embrace these principles. We have also been taught so by our parents and educators. But when questioned "how do you know it is so?", or "why must it be that way?", sincerely asked questions not from scoffers, we have difficulty answering, because we haven't delved into these firmly adhered to principles ourselves. If the inquirer is a young adult or teenager, the lack of a coherent answer to the question can be quite disturbing.

We are grateful and endorse the activities of Rav Dovid Sapirman and the Ani Maamin Foundation who have travelled extensively to teach and lecture and prove that these principles are logically immutable. Presently Rabbi Sapirman is writing and publishing a book based on these lectures to enable many more people to fulfill the precept of דע את אלקי אביך ועובדהו to be a *knowledgable* servant of הקב"ה.

We wish him success in this endeavour and through this book יתרבה ההכרה והדעת בהקב"ה.

With friendship and respect,

Yaakov Hirschman

Yaakov M. Hirschman

Table of Contents

Acknowledgments 13
Introduction 16

Part One: The Emunah Sugar Cube

Chapter One: Building a Strong Foundation 22
Chapter Two: What Is Emunah? 26
Chapter Three: Emunah Peshutah versus Blind Faith............................ 30

Part Two: Torah Min HaShamayim

Chapter Four: The Revelation at Har Sinai 38
Chapter Five: Our Claim Is Indeed True 51
Chapter Six: Well, Maybe It Happened Differently 58
Chapter Seven: What Could the Motive Be?.. 62
Chapter Eight: Other Beliefs: Unproved and Unprovable 67
Chapter Nine: Yetzias Mitzrayim — the Eternal Testimony 74
Chapter Ten: Who Wrote All This?... 80
Chapter Eleven: He Knows in Advance 89

Part Three: The Creator's Signature Is Everywhere

Chapter Twelve: The Awesome Creator 124
Chapter Thirteen: Know Who and What You Are Up Against............. 126
Chapter FourteenInvisible but Everywhere 128

Chapter Fifteen: Plan and Purpose 137
Chapter Sixteen: Tools and Accessories 141
Chapter Seventeen: Humans 152
Chapter Eighteen: A Deeper Look 158

Part Four: Evolution — You Be the Judge
Chapter Nineteen: The Essence of the Theory 166
Chapter Twenty: A Common Sense Approach 170
Chapter Twenty-one: Glaring Problems 176
Chapter Twenty-two: Some Things Just Don't Add Up 181
Chapter Twenty-three: Fossils 184
Chapter Twenty-four: More Proofs 188
Chapter Twenty-five: Creation Is Not on Their Radar 195
Chapter Twenty-six: G-d-Guided Evolution? 200
Chapter Twenty-seven: How Can People Be Oblivious to the Obvious Truth? 210
Chapter Twenty-eight: Please Don't Take My Word For It 215
Chapter Twenty-nine: The Emunah Sugar Cube 217

About the Author 221
Dedications 222

Acknowledgments

Completing this book has entailed a considerable investment of time and effort for over two years. When a person reaches a milestone, the very first thing to do is to express gratitude to the Ribono shel Olam for His benevolence. Just as the farmer who brings *bikkurim* and the person who eats a meal thanks Hashem not only for those fruits or for that particular meal, but for everything from *yetzias Mitzrayim* and on, so too must I be grateful to Him not only for this accomplishment, but for all the kindness He has bestowed on me throughout my life.

The Ribono shel Olam sends many messengers to do His bidding. My gratitude to these *shluchei d'Rachmana* cannot be sufficiently expressed.

Without the support and encouragement of my *eishes chayil, shetichyeh*, this book could never have become a reality. May she and I together be *zocheh* (in good health) to see true *Torahdike nachas* from all our children and grandchildren, *b'ezras Hashem*.

Mosaica Press has done an excellent and most professional job of turning a manuscript into a beautifully crafted book. Rabbi Haber and I have been friends for decades, and it is an honor to have been able to share this project with him. Rabbi Doron Kornbluth's insights and comments, as well as his exceptional patience, have made this project possible.

This book is merely one facet of the ongoing campaign of the Ani Maamin Foundation to strengthen *emunah* in *Klal Yisrael*. The Ribono shel Olam, in His infinite kindness, enabled me to establish the Ani Maamin Foundation over six years ago. Its aims include training *mechanchim* in the methodology to present *emunah* issues in a compelling manner, and to produce materials, both audio and written, to further this goal. This book is a part of that effort.

Our sincerest thanks to Leon and Simi Melohn for their vision and generosity in making this and future publications possible. May the Ribono shel Olam consider this a great and eternal *zechus* for their entire *mishpachah*.

Without the tireless efforts of Mr. Shlomo Szydlow (of Monsey), Ani Maamin would not even have been a dream. His passion, encouragement and advice were what enabled this organization to become an actual reality. May the *zechus* stand by him always, to see continued *nachas* from his entire *mishpachah*, and to always be involved in spreading *k'vod Shamayim* in the world.

My utmost thanks to the *Gedolei Yisrael* who have backed and encouraged us with their written *haskamos* and warm encouragement. They include HaRabbanim HaGaonim R. Shmuel Kaminetsky, R. Avrohom Chaim Levine, R. Aharon Feldman, R. Shlomo Miller and R. Moshe Mordechai Lowy, *shlita*.

It is an honor and a pleasure to work together with R. Pinchos Jung, who has lectured around the globe for Ani Maamin. I have learned so much from him and continue to bask in the warmth of his personality through my interactions with him on a daily basis.

Chaim Moore, director of our central office in Monsey, is the glue that holds together all the pieces of Ani Maamin. His efficiency, coupled with his dedication to our cause, are what makes it all happen.

Rabbi Moshe Pogrow, our executive director, has injected into our organization a new level of passion for our mission, combined with the dedication and know-how to make it happen. May Hashem grant him continued *hatzlachah*.

Aryeh Zev Narrow, executive director at the Rabbi Avigdor Miller Legacy Library/Simchas Hachaim Publishing has been a true and dedicated friend of Ani Maamin since its inception in ways too numerous to list. His efforts in disseminating the works of Rav Avigdor Miller, *zt"l*, go hand in hand with the aims and goals of Ani Maamin.

Acknowledgments 15

Special thanks to Dr. Jonathan Ostroff for the countless hours he spent with me working through the manuscript, in particular the section about evolution. Likewise, Rabbi Simcha Coffer gave much assistance and advice on that section of the book.

Rabbi Dovid Engel, Menahel of the Toronto Cheder, has enthusiastically embraced the work of Ani Maamin, used it in his Cheder, and continues to be a source of constant courage and inspiration. May he have continued success in his efforts for *harbotzas Torah*.

Rabbi Shlomo Noach Mandel has created a shul in Toronto that is most conducive to growth in *ruchniyus*. Our friendship and work together have spanned many decades. May he have ongoing success in his efforts for spreading Torah both in Toronto and across Eastern Europe.

Kollel Keser Torah, founded by the Rosh Kollel, R. Avraham Kahn, *shlita*, is a wonderful place to keep the fire of *ahavas Torah* burning. May the *kollel* continue to grow and serve as a great source of *chizuk* to its participants.

It is hard to find the right words to thank the people who have supported Ani Maamin with financial assistance over the last six years. May they have a share in the increased *chizuk* in *emunah* that they helped to establish.

The encouragement we have received from the over twelve thousand people who have heard our audio *emunah* presentations has given us the strength to persevere in the face of sometimes difficult odds.

Last, but not least, I once again thank the Ribono shel Olam for allowing me to have some small share in *kiddush Shem Shamayim*, and offer my fervent *tefillos* to Him to allow me to continue doing so for many long, productive years.

DS
Toronto, Canada

Introduction

This book is about the beliefs of the Jewish people. We call these beliefs *"emunah."* Undoubtedly, most observant Jews are *ma'aminim,* believers. After all, they were raised in homes where Torah ideals were accepted without reservations. A significant part of their lives may have been spent studying in a yeshiva or in a Bais Yaakov-type school. Their entire life cycle is regulated by the dictates of the Torah, from early morning until late at night: davening, learning and mitzvos. If they weren't really *ma'aminim,* would they live the way they do? If so, what need could such people have for a book about *emunah*?

Perhaps, however, there is a reality that even genuine *ma'aminim* sometimes face. Unless a conscious effort is made to keep *emunah* fresh and vibrant, one can easily slip into a pattern of just going through the motions, but without the sense of conviction that ought to be there. In that case, this book may prove to be an eye-opener.

Most people who subscribe to the Torah tradition were educated from earliest childhood to believe in it. Judaism was presented to them as a matter of fact — an absolute reality. Unfortunately, however, many observant Jews may never have advanced past the simplistic version of their faith presented to them in their youth. These matters may never have been discussed, either at home or in their schools.

As a result, it may be difficult for an individual to articulate to himself the fundamentals of *emunah.* This makes it harder to summon the strength and sense of security that would be so helpful in shielding oneself from the skepticism of the society that surrounds us and the constant bombardment of alien values that come to us from the media. Someone without this clarity of conviction is unlikely to daven with great *kavanah* or succeed in transmitting a deep sense of *emunah* to his or her children.

Even someone who seeks *chizuk* and clarity in areas of *emunah* may sometimes be deterred by the fear of being looked down upon for raising such questions. That is why it is so important to discuss these things openly, and find the clarity already available in the teachings of our *sefarim*.

LIVING BY OUR ETERNAL FAITH

Klal Yisrael has remained steadfast in its faith in the Ribono shel Olam for over three thousand years. Through fire and water, we have held on tenaciously to our belief in the Creator and His Torah. Countless Jews have allowed themselves to be martyred *al kiddush Hashem* rather than to even pretend to accept a foreign belief. We are proud to bear the title "*ma'aminim b'nei ma'aminim*."

Our beliefs can and should have an incredible impact on our everyday lives. Yet, for many observant Jews, although we are all *ma'aminim b'nei ma'aminim*, our *emunah* doesn't always influence our everyday decisions in a significant way. But when the *emunah* is clear, compelling and vibrant, then it certainly will affect our daily lives. Hence, there can hardly be anything more fundamental to proper observance of Torah than gaining clarity in *emunah*. The *navi* told us this idea ages ago.

> מכות כד
> בא חבקוק והעמידן על אחת שנאמר (חבקוק ב') וצדיק באמונתו יחיה.
>
> Then (the navi) Chavakuk came along and established all six hundred and thirteen mitzvos on one principle: "The tzaddik lives by his emunah."

This passage in the Gemara means that originally, every one of the mitzvos served as a gateway to perfection in keeping the entire Torah. As time went on and the spiritual stature of the generations declined, the number of these gateways diminished. In this verse, the *navi* Chavakuk told us that the only remaining gateway to the full, proper observance of all 613 mitzvos is through *emunah*. There is no way around this. It has to start with *emunah*.

Even people who already have such genuine *emunah* need regular *chizuk*. Given the society in which we live, the influences to which we are exposed constantly, and the temptations we must withstand, few things could be more important than intensifying the conviction that our *emunah* is the absolute and sole truth on earth. When we gain a heightened sense of clarity in the belief in a *Borei Olam,* Who gave us His written and oral Torah, we will be able to acquire the value system to love and live by the *derech Hashem.*

OF COURSE WE BELIEVE — BUT DO WE?

Let me share with you an enlightening experience. While working in *kiruv rechokim* (outreach), I encountered a certain fine young man who became very serious about keeping *Yiddishkeit* and mitzvos. His parents, quite alarmed, called me and requested a meeting. (I'm still not sure what help they thought I would be to them, but I agreed to the meeting anyway.)

They asked me, "Rabbi, why can't he compromise?" I knew just what they meant: On Monday we'll serve him kosher, but on Tuesday let him come to the Chinese restaurant with us. Let him keep this Shabbos, but next week, when we have a family outing, why can't he come along? I answered them, "Your son believes that G-d gave us the Torah. Someone who believes that G-d gave the Torah can't compromise." The poor woman got the most puzzled look on her face I have ever seen. She turned to her husband in utter bewilderment and said, "Well! We believe that G-d gave the Torah, don't we David?" Whereupon he answered, with the same puzzled look on his face, "I don't know, dear, do we?"

These people were educated professionals, members of a Conservative synagogue, so-called intellectuals. Yet they had never taken the time to decide whether they do believe in a G-d-given Torah or not.

This episode was an eye-opener for me. Not only was I amazed about that particular couple, but it made me realize that perhaps many of us *frum* Jews actually do the very same thing. We go through the motions and hardly ever stop to analyze what precisely it is that we believe in, and what should be the resultant consequences of these beliefs on our lives.

THIS BOOK

This book has been deliberately written in simple language so as to make it comfortable for young readers as well as old. It can be used by private individuals or as a guide for a curriculum in a classroom. The manuscript is already in use in a number of high school classrooms both here and abroad. Either way, it is our hope that whoever uses it will discover a new sense of inspiration and excitement to possess a faith that is so compelling and so obviously true. It combines a lucid narrative, with the original sources from *gedolei Rishonim* and *Acharonim* woven into the text. Each source has been translated for the convenience of the reader. These sources emanate from the pure hearts of these great writers, and we know very well that words that come forth from the heart will enter the heart. May it be the will of Hashem Yisborach that our *emunah* will indeed be strengthened, and we will, as the *navi* said, "Live by our *emunah*."

PART ONE

THE EMUNAH SUGAR CUBE

CHAPTER ONE

Building a Strong Foundation

*I*magine trying to build a skyscraper (or even a plain one-story house) without first laying down a foundation. After a while, the ground underneath will shift, the doors and windows will not open and close properly, and eventually the whole house may crumble.

In Judaism, as well, we need a strong foundation upon which to build. Eventually, our building will be many stories high. However, if we try to build the upper floors before we have the foundation, then our spiritual doors and windows won't open and close properly. We may be unhappy, unfulfilled, and some may even be looking for an exit out of this crooked building.

WHAT IS THE FOUNDATION?

There is no question as to what the foundation of *Yiddishkeit* is. It is *emunah*. In order for all the higher levels to fit into place and function as they should, we first have to know without the slightest doubt that the belief system we inherited from our parents, teachers and all previous generations is one hundred percent unadulterated truth. It isn't the product of someone's imagination, these aren't stories that were fabricated somewhere over a moonlit campfire; this is the simple plain truth. Although there are many more vital concepts, three will suffice to begin the process.

1. There is a *Borei Olam*. He really exists, created everything and maintains everything by His will;
2. He spoke to the entire Jewish people at Har Sinai and gave us His Torah;
3. This Torah was given in two parts: one written and one oral. After acquiring these three fundamental beliefs, we will be able to begin building, *b'ezras Hashem*.

HOW EMPTY WITHOUT EMUNAH

Emunah is indeed wonderful for those who possess it. We live in a world where so many people suffer from depression, or at least a deep sense of frustration, caused by a sense of meaninglessness. Unfortunately, there is good reason for their feelings. In a society that is mostly atheistic and subscribes to the theory of evolution, there isn't that much to feel good about.

After all, if life is just haphazard, the result of nothing more than chance, what intrinsic value does any individual have? What meaning does someone's existence have if he was born by sheer luck to be a member of a species that just happened to evolve from sub-humans? What difference will it make in the greater scheme of things when he leaves the world through bad luck or sheer chance?

HOW PRECIOUS TO BELIEVE

Not so the believer. For him, the universe is a very different place. He knows that there is a Creator who made the world according to His master plan. He gave us His manual for successful life, His Torah. By following the instructions in the manual, he can live a decent, harmonious and inspiring life. A believer formulates his world view based on information given to us by the Creator Himself. However, no matter how beneficial belief may be, it doesn't make one a believer unless he is actually convinced that he has hit upon the truth.

This is my sincere hope in presenting this book to the reader: that in some small way the reader will feel more confident in his belief in Torah and experience the great feeling of knowing that life has a plan and a purpose, and that each individual has a significant role to play.

WHAT EMUNAH CAN DO FOR YOU

Emunah is the sugar cube that sweetens the coffee and turns it into a delicious drink. When it is clear to you that your existence here is not haphazard, but rather with plan and purpose, then you will be able to experience a passionate *simchas ha-chaim*. You will know that you can accomplish the mission you were put here to fulfill (even if the ride is sometimes bumpy). After that, an even better World awaits you, one so marvelous that humans cannot comprehend it during their physical existence.

Every mitzvah you do is accredited to your *Olam Haba* account, and no *tefillah* goes for naught. Everything that happens in the world has been engineered for your maximum benefit, even when you don't understand how or why. Concurrently, the Torah way of life allows you to enjoy the pleasures of this world, and utilize them as fuel to accomplish the ultimate purpose of life. The beginning of all this great fortune is when a person knows that the Torah is indeed the word of Hashem.

Perhaps the reader may say, "I already believe in Hashem and His Torah. I already have the foundation. Am I not ready for the next levels?" Superficial belief is not enough. A foundation must be 100 percent solid. One must be totally convinced. Before we can absorb the higher concepts, we must know and feel with every fiber of our being that the *Borei Olam* exists, and that the *Chumash* is nothing less than a letter to *Klal Yisrael* collectively and to you personally. He must also know, without a shadow of a doubt, that the *Chumash* is only a small part of a very long letter, with the *Torah she-b'al peh* constituting its main part. Then you will not need to grope in the dark. The Torah will become your frame of reference, the source to which you turn for life instructions. The *chachmei haTorah*, who have transmitted the Oral Torah in an unbroken chain from Moshe Rabbeinu down to us, will be your mentors. When all this is as clear to you as it is that you have two hands with five fingers on each, then indeed you will be ready to proceed.

As we have said, going through the motions without this clarity will not inspire you. Knowing, understanding, and sincerely believing and trusting in Hashem most certainly will.

CHAPTER TWO

What Is Emunah?

TO REALLY KNOW, NOT JUST BELIEVE

Agreeing to believe is not believing. You cannot sign a contract to believe. Either you really believe or you don't. Just because we are determined to remain *frum* doesn't mean we are actually convinced. The mitzvah of *emunah* requires us to believe with such solid clarity that we don't just believe, but rather we know. We know there is a Creator. We know that He gave us His Torah. This is how the Torah expresses the mitzvah of *emunah* in various places.

"I AM HASHEM, YOUR G-D"

The mitzvah of *Anochi Hashem,* at the beginning of the Ten Commandments, is considered by most of the *Rishonim* to be the mitzvah to believe.[1] The *Sefer Hachinuch* tells us what constitutes proper *emunah*.

> וענין האמונה הוא שיקבע בנפשו שהאמת כן ושאי אפשר בחילוף זה בשום פנים ואם ישאל עליו ישיב לכל שואל שזה יאמין לבו ולא יודע בחילוף זה אפילו יאמרו להרגו:

---

1 Others say that it is so fundamental, it comes before the 613.

> **ספר החינוך, מצוה כה**
>
> The idea of this emunah is that he should affix in his nefesh that this is the truth (that there is a Creator), and that anything to the contrary is absolutely impossible. Should he be asked about this, he will answer to any questioner that this is what he believes, and he would never admit to the contrary, even if they say they will kill him.

Nothing less than feeling that the contrary is impossible will do. In other contexts, as well, we are commanded not just to believe, but rather to know.

> **דברים ד, לט**
>
> וידעת היום והשבת אל לבבך כי ד' הוא האלקים בשמים ממעל ועל הארץ מתחת אין עוד:
>
> You shall know today and turn it over into your heart that Hashem is G-d in the heavens above and on the earth below. There is none other.

> **דברים ז, ט**
>
> וידעת כי ד' אלקיך הוא האלקים הק-ל הנאמן שמר הברית והחסד לאהביו ולשמרי מצותיו לאלף דור:
>
> You shall know that Hashem, your G-d, is the (only) G-d, the trustworthy G-d, who keeps the covenant and His kindness, to those who love Him and to those who keep His mitzvos, for a thousand generations.

> **דברים כט, ה**
>
> לחם לא אכלתם ויין ושכר לא שתיתם למען תדעו כי אני ד' אלקיכם:
>
> You didn't eat bread or drink intoxicating wine (in the desert when you ate only mann and drank from the spring in the stone) in order that you shall know that I am Hashem your G-d.

Right from the start, even before we were taken from bondage in Mitzrayim, we were told what it means to have *emunah*.

> **שמות ו, ז**
>
> ולקחתי אתכם לי לעם והייתי לכם לאלקים וידעתם כי אני ד' אלקיכם המוציא אתכם מתחת סבלות מצרים:
>
> *I will take you to Me for a nation and you shall know that I am Hashem, your G-d, who brings you out from beneath the burdens of Egypt.*

> **שמות י, ב**
>
> ולמען תספר באזני בנך ובן בנך את אשר התעללתי במצרים ואת אתתי אשר שמתי בם וידעתם כי אני ד':
>
> *In order that you shall tell in the ears of your son and your grandson how I made a joke out of Egypt, and My signs that I put among them, and you shall know that I am Hashem.*

The Rambam begins his *sefer* with the mitzvah of knowing the existence of the Creator.[2]

> **רמב"ם - הלכות יסודי התורה פרק א הלכה א**
>
> יסוד היסודות ועמוד החכמות לידע שיש שם מצוי ראשון, והוא ממציא כל נמצא, וכל הנמצאים משמים וארץ ומה שביניהם לא נמצאו אלא מאמתת המצאו.
>
> *The foundation of all foundations is to know that there is One who always existed, and who caused all that is to come into being. All that exists in the heavens and the earth and all that is between them only exists as a result of the truth of His existence.*

---

[2] רמב"ם - הלכות יסודי התורה פרק א: א יסוד היסודות ועמוד החכמות לידע שיש שם מצוי ראשון, והוא ממציא כל נמצא, וכל הנמצאים משמים וארץ ומה שביניהם לא נמצאו אלא מאמתת המצאו. ב ואם יעלה על הדעת שהוא אינו מצוי אין דבר אחר יכול להמצאות. ג ואם יעלה על הדעת שאין כל הנמצאים מלבדו מצויים הוא לבדו יהיה מצוי, ולא יבטל הוא לבטולם, שכל הנמצאים צריכין לו והוא ברוך הוא אינו צריך להם ולא לאחד מהם, לפיכך אין אמתתו כאמתת אחד מהם. ד הוא שהנביא אומר וד' אלוקים אמת, הוא לבדו האמת ואין לאחר אמת כאמתתו, והוא שהתורה אומרת אין עוד מלבדו, כלומר אין שם מצוי אמת מלבדו כמותו. ה המצוי הזה הוא אלוקי העולם אדון כל הארץ, והוא המנהיג הגלגל בכח שאין לו קץ ותכלית, בכח שאין לו הפסק, שהגלגל סובב תמיד ואי אפשר שיסוב בלא מסבב, והוא ברוך הוא המסבב אותו בלא יד ובלא גוף. ו וידיעת דבר זה מצות עשה שנאמר אנכי ד' אלוקיך, וכל המעלה על דעתו שיש שם אלוה אחר חוץ מזה, עובר בלא תעשה שנאמר לא יהיה לך אלוקים אחרים על פני, וכופר בעיקר שזהו העיקר הגדול שהכל תלוי בו.

From all of the above we have learned that one who merely subscribes to or accepts our belief has not done the *emunah* justice. One has to know with every fiber of his being that this is all true, to the point that "it is impossible to be otherwise."

CHAPTER THREE

Emunah Peshutah versus Blind Faith

We call a faith that is equivalent to "knowing," *emunah peshutah*, simple faith. With *emunah peshutah*, one has no doubts and feels no need to question. How does one arrive at *emunah peshutah*? There are two valid ways in which to do this. The first is called *kabbalas Avos*, where we rely on the historical tradition we have received from our predecessors. We have no doubts about our beliefs, because we know we have received them from totally reliable sources. The second is called *emunas ha-seichel*, which means that we came to believe through our own intellect and common sense.

KABBALAS AVOS

We have an amazing heritage that has been transmitted to us from the generations that came before us. For over three thousand years, *Klal Yisrael* has delved into every nuance of our Torah. Not only have they pondered its laws and all their implications, but also our claims and beliefs. Our leaders and scholars were not only the most righteous of people, but also possessed the greatest minds. These geniuses analyzed our faith from every possible angle. Had there been a single flaw in it, they surely would have found it. But no! They believed wholeheartedly in the Torah, because they understood that it is 100 percent true.

We can say with absolute certainty that if Rabbi Akiva, Rav Ashi, Rashi, the Rambam, the Vilna Gaon and the Chofetz Chaim believed in Hashem and His Torah, you can be sure they didn't miss a loophole. This alone is sufficient to allow us to rely confidently on the *mesorah*.

Someone who relies on this *mesorah* has a belief based on *kabbalas Avos*. Although this person didn't work through the substantiation himself, he is confident it is true because of the integrity of his sources. He doesn't doubt the honesty of his parents and teachers, who link him back to all the above-mentioned giants of spirit and intellect. As far as he is concerned, he has been taught the truth, has no need for further substantiation, and that is good enough for him. For anyone who has this trust, this will suffice, and indeed this person has one type of *emunah peshutah*.

EMUNAS HA-SEICHEL

There is another method to achieve *emunah peshutah*. When we engage our intellect to review the *mesorah* with an objective eye, we will see that it is ironclad, virtually incontrovertible. We will know without a shadow of a doubt that "Moshe is true and his Torah is true." This knowledge will excite and inspire us to live according to the instructions of the Torah with a sense of honor and pride.

This faith-strengthening process of working through the *emunah* with our own intellect is beneficial and recommended for all people, even for those who are already convinced by virtue of what they have received in the *mesorah*. Substantiating *emunah* with one's own *seichel* offers an advantage not available through *kabbalas Avos*. It provides an excitement — a passion and an enthusiasm that make the *emunah* alive and vibrant.

HOW TO ARRIVE AT EMUNAS HA-SEICHEL

We can arrive at the fundamentals of our *emunah* with plain common sense. No magical "leap of faith" is necessary in order to believe. All we need is to use our own minds objectively. The fundamentals are actually so self-evident that after delving into them ourselves, we will look on in amazement at someone who does not believe. How can they possibly not see that this is the plain truth? That's actually what this book is all about: coming to realize how logical it is to believe, and how senseless it is not to believe. As we progress, we shall perceive with our own minds, *b'ezras Hashem*, that the collective parents and teachers of all previous generations knew exactly what they were talking about. They didn't transmit a fable, a *bubba maaseh*, or a product of someone's imagination. When we finish this process, we will have gained a new reverence for the *mesorah*, realizing that what was transmitted to us was true all along. This is called *emunas ha-seichel*, and complements *kabbalas Avos*. It is highly preferable to have the combination of *mesorah* and *seichel*, as advocated by many *gedolim*. This is what the Ba'al Shem Tov had to say on the matter:

> **מובא בספר בעל שם טוב על התורה דף קעו**
>
> טעם למה אנו אומרים אלקינו ואלקי אבותינו כי יש שני סוגי בני אדם המאמינים בהשם יתברך. א' שמאמין בהקדוש ברוך הוא מחמת שהולך בדרכי אבותיו הקדמונים ועם כל זה אמונתו חזקה והב' הוא מי שבא על האמנת הדת מחמת החקירה והחילוק ביניהם הוא שהסוג הא' יש לו מעלה שאי אפשר לפתות אותו אף אם יאמרו לו כמה חקירות הסותרות ח"ו כי אמונתו חזקה מצד קבלת אבותיו ועוד שלא חקר מעולם אבל יש לו חסרון שהאמונה אצלו רק מצות אנשים מלומדה בלי טעם ושכל אבל הב' יש לו מעלה שמחמת שהכיר הבורא יתברך מחמת גודל חקירתו הוא חזק באמונה שלימה ובאהבה גמורה אבל גם כן יש לו חסרון שבקל יכולים לפתותו ואם יביאו לו ראיות הסותרות חקירותיו יתפתה ח"ו אבל מי ששני המדות בידו אין למעלה הימנו דהיינו שסומך על אבותיו הקדמונים בחוזק וגם כן בא לו על ידי שחקר בעצמו זו היא אמונה שלימה וטובה ולזה אנו אומרים אלקינו ואלקי אבותינו וכו'.

The reason that we say "our G-d and the G-d of our fathers" is that there are two types of people that believe in Hashem Yisborach.

1. *He believes in Hakadosh Baruch Hu because he follows in the ways of his forefathers, and still his emunah is strong.*
2. *He comes to believe in our Torah from his own intellectual investigation.*

The difference between them is that the person from the first category has an advantage that he cannot be convinced to give up his emunah, even if they bring him many proofs that contradict it, chas v'shalom. His emunah

> remains strong because it comes from what he received from his forefathers, and because he himself never delved into intellectual investigations. However, it has a shortcoming that his emunah is by rote, without reason and seichel. The second group, however, has an advantage. Since he recognized the Creator through much contemplation, his emunah is total and with complete love (of Hashem), but it also has a disadvantage. It is easy to convince this person to forsake the emunah if they bring him proofs which contradict his investigations. The person who has both methods is the highest ma'aminim of all. He relies completely on what he received from his Avos, but also has worked out the emunah in his own seichel. That is the good and complete emunah. That is why we say, "Our G-d, and the G-d of our fathers."

In our cynical, skeptical generation, there are many people who do not have such unshakable faith in their parents, teachers, or even the great *chachamim* of yesteryear, to rely on the faith of *kabbalas Avos*. They want proof and don't want to be told to rely on someone else for a belief system which is to be the basis of everything they will do throughout their entire lives. For them to acquire this simple, unquestioning faith requires them to first work through the *emunah* with their own common sense. They have to start with *emunas ha-seichel*. When they work through it, they will realize retroactively that what was transmitted to them in the *mesorah* is actually the absolute truth. Of course, not everything can be understood with our own minds. If, after working through the basic fundamentals, there remain some conceptual details that are beyond our ability to grasp, we can and should rely on the *mesorah*, because we know that it is from Hashem.

This idea is found in the writings of the Maharsha:[3]

> מהרש"א ברכות יז. בא"ד גמור
> דחייב כל אדם להשכיל בידיעת מציאותו ואחדותו ויכלתו וידיעת דרכיו כו'
> ית' כפי יד שכלו של אדם אך על פי אמונתנו והתורה וכל מה שנראה לו
> בשכלו שהוא נגד תורתנו הקדושה לא יאמין בו רק יתלה הדבר בקט שכלו כו'.

---

3   The Maharsha is addressing here even people who have solid *emunah* based on what they received from their parents and teachers. In a short pamphlet I wrote, I quoted from many other *gedolim* who state that everyone should substantiate the *emunah* with their *seichel*, even if they are already totally convinced by *kabbalas Avos*.

> *A person is obligated to use his logic to know Hashem Yisborach's existence, Oneness and ability, etc., as much as the person's seichel can grasp. But this must be done according to our emunah and our Torah. Whatever seems to his seichel against our Holy Torah he should not believe in it, but rather assume that the error is coming from the limitations of his mind.*

BLIND FAITH

Some people think that being a *ma'amin* requires them to shut off their minds and simply accept whatever they have been told, without thinking and without questioning.[4] This, they think, is what we refer to by the term *emunah peshutah*, simple faith. What a terrible misconception! A person who believes without any logical reason to do so, does not have *emunah peshutah* at all, but rather a blind, senseless faith.

Imagine that you are sniffling and coughing with a cold, on your way to a doctor's office. A well-dressed young man comes up to you, holding a doctor's satchel. A friendly type, he says, "Oh! I see you have a cold." You respond that such is indeed the case, and you are currently on the way to your doctor on the other side of town. He tells you it's your lucky day, because he is a doctor and can save you the trip. He pulls out a tongue depressor and wants to look at your throat. Although you resist, he is very insistent, and finally you agree, rather than argue with him. "Oh, yes! It's quite inflamed. Here! Take this prescription and you'll be fine soon enough." He hands you a prescription, says good bye and leaves. Do you fill that prescription? Why should you, when you have no basis on which to take his word? He may be a quack or an impostor. Trusting him would be blind faith. You will have put your trust in someone without having any real reason to do so, simply because he looks legitimate. Remember, blind faith means that one puts his trust in something without having a logical reason to do so.

Someone who says he believes in Hashem and the Torah only because he was brought up to be *frum*, and these are the things *frum* people believe,

---

4   Later on, we will see that other religions actually rely on blind faith, with no intellectual basis whatsoever.

has a very watered-down type of *emunah*. He isn't saying that he relies on the truth of the message he received from his parents and teachers, with no doubts whatsoever about its veracity. He also isn't saying that he worked it through and sees it is the truth. He is really saying: I don't know anything else. This is what I was brought up with, this is what my family does, so I will just stay with it. Even if he says he believes in what Judaism teaches, and maybe even really means it, it's simply not more than blind faith, at best.

This is not similar to the *emunah* that this author saw among his peers fifty years ago. When a *bachur* said then that he believes in Hashem or His Torah because his father or *rebbi* told him, he meant to say that he was totally confident that they had transmitted the truth to him. That was *kabbalas Avos*.

What *emunah peshutah* really means is that a person is so totally convinced that what he believes in is true that he has no further need for any substantiation. His belief is as clear to him as the *pashut* (simple) fact that two plus two equals four. Even the *emunah* of *kabbalas Avos* requires one to analyze the *mesorah* enough to realize that it can be totally relied upon for accuracy and integrity. This is not blind at all — quite the opposite!

The Jewish people's belief in Torah is not based on blind faith — not at all. Yes, we do believe unquestioningly. However, we do not fill the prescription before we first check out the doctor's credentials (or rely on others whom we completely trust to check him out for us). We think and examine. We know that we haven't been taken in by some sort of hoax, because our *mesorah* can be traced back until we see that it is incontrovertible fact. Pure logic — and plain common sense — force us to conclude that the fundamental axioms of Judaism are true. There is no alternative. In other words, *emunah peshutah* means that a person has attained such confidence in the honesty and accuracy of the source from which he received the *emunah* that he has no doubts and feels no further need to question.

When we have achieved this, we possess the *emunah* sugar cube.

PART TWO
TORAH MIN HASHAMAYIM

CHAPTER FOUR

The Revelation at Har Sinai

A ll of Judaism revolves around the idea that the Creator revealed Himself to us at Sinai. When this is clear to us, every word and every letter of Torah is of infinite significance, because it is the *d'var Hashem*. Without this knowledge, Torah is perceived as merely the teachings of some person (or group of people), somewhere, sometime.

We know for sure that our faith is true because Hashem spoke to us at Mount Sinai directly, in such a manner as to leave no room for doubt. Hence, everything we find in the Torah is eternally true, and of phenomenal importance. Even perceiving the existence of the Creator, (which can be demonstrated by other methods), can be arrived at as a result of the Revelation at Sinai. After all, if Hashem spoke to us there, He obviously exists!

Therefore, we will begin by first substantiating the *emunah* in *ma'amad Har Sinai*. Subsequently, we will return to the subject of substantiating the existence of the Creator directly.[5]

---

5   Generally, in presentations such as this book, the existence of the Creator is dealt with first, followed by the substantiation of the Revelation at Sinai. For a variety of reasons, I have chosen to reverse the order here. The existence of a Creator can certainly be shown by establishing the historicity of the Revelation. The direct presentation of *metzius Haborei*, will follow in Part Three of this book.

OUR CLAIM

In a free society, anyone may claim anything he wants. If someone desires to claim that he is Napoleon or George Washington, it's not against the law. True, no sensible person will pay attention, but, nevertheless, he is free to make reckless, silly claims. A person can even say that he is the Mashiach without fear of punishment! While a person may claim anything, before we can decide whether or not to believe the claim, we need to do some careful analysis.

Judaism makes very distinct and daring claims, vastly different from anything claimed by any other religion. We claim that the Creator of the universe spoke directly to our ancestors (about three million of them) at Har Sinai. Every single man, woman and child was included in the prophecy. Before that, G-d Himself performed stupendous miracles for our *Avos* in Mitzrayim and in the desert. There were ten miraculous plagues, the splitting of the Red Sea, the falling of the *mann* from the sky every day and the miraculous well that traveled along with them to supply them with water wherever they encamped. A pillar of cloud guided them by day and a pillar of fire by night.

All these miracles and many additional ones took place publicly. No one needed to be convinced, because everyone saw the miracles personally. This is our claim and has always been the claim of the Jewish people.[6] It is important to know that there is no other nation or religion that even claims anything remotely similar.

Mainstream Jewry never had another version. Jewish groups that claimed anything contrary to our *mesorah* arose much later, and attempted to rewrite history.[7] They had no historical tradition and no chain of eyewitness testimony. They simply presented whatever suited their agenda as the history of the Jewish people.

---

6   The Christian religion, which officially believes in what they call the Old Testament, fully agrees to the story of the Revelation and everything in the Hebrew Bible. They merely say that G-d subsequently changed His mind, discarded us and chose them. Islam agrees to the Revelation at Sinai, but says that we altered some parts of the Biblical narrative to discredit them. This is absurd, however, because the Torah scrolls were in existence for seventeen hundred years before the advent of Islam.

7   That is precisely what the *Tzedukim* did with regard to *Torah She-b'al Peh*. In more recent times, the Reform and Conservative movements have also reinterpreted history to suit their agenda.

SEFER HACHINUCH[8]

The *Sefer Hachinuch* begins with this very idea. After telling us that all societies recognize the validity of eyewitness testimony (including our Holy Torah), he makes the following fundamental statement:

> **הקדמה לספר החינוך**
>
> על כן כשרצה האלקים לתת תורה לעמו ישראל נתנה להם לעיני שש מאות אלף אנשים גדולים מלבד טף ונשים רבים להיות כולם עדים נאמנים על הדברים. גם למען תהיה העדות יותר חזקה זכו כלם למעלת הנבואה לפי שאין במה שיודע מצד הנבואה נופל ספק לעולם. וזהו שאמר השם יתברך למשה בעבור ישמע העם בדברי עמך וגם בך יאמינו לעולם כלומר הם ובניהם לעולם יאמינו בך ובנבואתך כי אז ידעו ידיעה נאמנה כי ידבר אלקים את האדם וחי ושכל נבואתך אמת.
>
> אבל אחרי הנבואה לא נשאר להם שום צד פקפוק בענין וידעו בברור כי כל המעשים נעשו במצות אדון העולם ומידו הגיע אליהם הכל והם שראו בעיניהם וידעו הדבר ידיעה אמיתית שאין לבני האדם אמת יותר חזקה מזה העידו לבניהם אשר ילדו אחרי כן כי כל דברי התורה אשר קבלו על ידי משה מ"בראשית" עד "לעיני כל ישראל" אמת וברור בלי שום ספק בעולם ובניהם העידו לבניהם גם כן ובניהם לבניהם עדיין נמצאת תורתנו בידינו מפי שש מאות אלף עדים נאמנים.

Therefore, when Hashem wanted to give the Torah to His people Yisrael, He gave it to them before the eyes of six hundred thousand adult men, besides many women and children, that they shall all be trustworthy witnesses on these matters. Also, in order that the testimony shall be all the stronger, all of them were privileged to receive prophecy. No doubt can ever arise on whatever is made known through prophecy. This is what Hashem said to Moshe, "In order that the nation will hear when I speak to you, and they will believe in you forever." This means to say: They and their children will believe in you and your prophecy forever, for then they will know with certain knowledge that G-d speaks with mankind and (the person) continues to live, and that all your prophecy is truth. But after the prophecy, there remained not the slightest possibility of doubt, and they knew clearly that all the events had taken place by the command of the Master of the world, and had all come to them directly from His hand. They, who saw with their own eyes and knew it to be perfectly true (for no

---

8 The *Sefer Hachinuch* is a classical work about the six hundred and thirteen mitzvos, written by a student of Ramban, exact authorship unknown.

> one can have a stronger knowledge of the truth than this was), testified to their children who were born afterward that all the words of the Torah which they had received from the hands of Moshe, from "Bereishis" until "l'einei kol Yisrael" are true and clear without any doubt in the world. Their children testified as well to their own children, and they to theirs until it reached us. So we discover that the Torah we have in our hands comes to us through the testimony of six hundred thousand witnesses.

THIS IS THE FOUNDATION

This is the basis for the mitzvos and all of Judaism. We all saw, we all heard, and each generation passed it on to the next. The Torah repeats this idea over and over again because it is so fundamental. It is what divides our faith from all others, *l'havdil*. The entire Jewish people personally witnessed all the miraculous things that took place in Mitzrayim, by *matan Torah* and in the *midbar*. None of these things occurred secretly or in private. All the plagues were done publicly to the *Mitzri'im*, and hence were known to all of *Bnei Yisrael*, who did not suffer from any of the *makkos*. The *krias Yam Suf*, as well, was an open, public demonstration.

The Torah was given to the first generation, which experienced everything personally. Hashem Yisborach expected us to keep all His mitzvos because we knew first hand that the Torah is all true. After all, we ourselves experienced everything. We didn't need to be forced, cursed or threatened into accepting this belief.[9] We simply knew that it was true, because we had seen it all ourselves. Then we handed down this information to our children and grandchildren in an unbroken chain. We will soon substantiate this claim, but we already see a major, significant difference between our claim and the claims of others. We will quote only a few of the many *pesukim* that state this openly.

When Moshe Rabbeinu first appeared to the people, Aharon was his spokesman. He performed the signs Hashem had given him publicly. They believed immediately:

---

9 It is true that the *Torah* prescribes punishments for transgressing, but never for lack of belief. Belief was not an issue for them.

> שמות ד' פסוק ל'-ל"א
>
> וידבר אהרן את כל הדברים אשר דבר ד' אל משה ויעש האתת לעיני העם: ויאמן העם וישמעו כי פקד ד' את בני ישראל וכי ראה את ענים ויקדו וישתחוו:
>
> And Aharon spoke all these words that Hashem had spoken to Moshe, and he did the signs before the eyes of the people. The people believed and understood that Hashem had remembered Bnei Yisrael and seen their affliction. They kneeled and bowed.[10]

The plagues affected only the *Mitzri'im*, not *Bnei Yisrael*. The following is one example of many:

> שמות י' פסוק כ"ב - כ"ג
>
> ויט משה את ידו על השמים ויהי חשך אפלה בכל ארץ מצרים שלשת ימים: לא ראו איש את אחיו ולא קמו איש מתחתיו שלשת ימים ולכל בני ישראל היה אור במושבתם:
>
> Moshe stretched out his hand to the heaven, and there was pitch darkness in the land of Mitzrayim for three days. No man could see his brother, nor rise up from his place for three days. But for all Bnei Yisrael there was light in their dwelling places.

At the Seder on Pesach night we transmit this to our children:

> דברים ו' פסוק כ' - כ"ב
>
> כי ישאלך בנך מחר לאמר מה העדת והחקים והמשפטים אשר צוה ד' אלקינו אתכם: ואמרת לבנך עבדים היינו לפרעה במצרים ויציאנו ד' ממצרים ביד חזקה: ויתן ד' אותת ומפתים גדלים ורעים במצרים בפרעה ובכל ביתו לעינינו:
>
> When your son will ask you in the future, saying, "What are the testimonies, the statutes and the judgments which your G-d commanded you?" You shall say to him, "We were slaves to Pharaoh in Egypt, and Hashem took us out from Egypt with a strong hand. Hashem gave great and terrible signs and wonders on Mitzrayim, on Pharaoh and all his household before our eyes."

---

10   The Torah never tells us to believe because of these signs. After all, they were not performed in front of all six hundred thousand people. They were used only as a first introduction for the people who witnessed them. We merely cite them here to show that from the very beginning, Moshe (and Aharon) substantiated their claims with open demonstrations.

Moshe Rabbeinu reminds them constantly that they saw everything personally:

> **דברים כ"ט פסוק א - ב**
>
> ויקרא משה אל כל ישראל ויאמר אלהם אתם ראיתם את כל אשר עשה ד' לעיניכם בארץ מצרים לפרעה ולכל עבדיו ולכל ארצו: המסות הגדלת אשר ראו עיניך האתת והמפתים הגדלים ההם:
>
> *Moshe called all of Yisrael and said to them, "You have seen all that Hashem did before your eyes in the land of Mitzrayim, to Pharaoh, to all his servants and all his land. The great tests that your eyes saw, those great signs and wonders."*

Moshe Rabbeinu reviews for them many of the miracles they personally witnessed.

> **דברים י"א פסוק ב' - ז**
>
> וידעתם היום כי לא את בניכם אשר לא ידעו ואשר לא ראו את מוסר ד' אלקיכם את גדלו את ידו החזקה וזרעו הנטויה: ואת אתתיו ואת מעשיו אשר עשה בתוך מצרים לפרעה מלך מצרים ולכל ארצו: ואשר עשה לחיל מצרים לסוסיו ולרכבו אשר הציף את מי ים סוף על פניהם ברדפם אחריכם ויאבדם ד' עד היום הזה: ואשר עשה לכם במדבר עד באכם עד המקום הזה: ואשר עשה לדתן ולאבירם בני אליאב בן ראובן אשר פצתה הארץ את פיה ותבלעם ואת בתיהם ואת אהליהם ואת כל היקום אשר ברגליהם בקרב כל ישראל: כי עיניכם הראת את כל מעשה ד' הגדל אשר עשה:
>
> *You shall know today that I do not speak with your children who did not know and did not see the chastisement of Hashem, your G-d; His greatness, His strong hand and His outstretched arm; His signs and His deeds that He did among Egypt, to Pharoah, king of Egypt and to all his land. And what He did to the army of Mitzrayim, their horses and chariots, that he flooded the waters of the Yam Suf on their faces when they chased after you. Hashem destroyed them until this very day. And what He did for you in the desert until you came to this place. And what He did to Dasan and Aviram the sons of Eliav, that the earth opened up its mouth and swallowed them and their houses and their tents and all the property that was with them, among all Israel. Rather, it was your own eyes that saw all the great deeds that Hashem did.*

Bnei Yisrael saw the cloud of the Divine Presence constantly and clearly throughout the forty years:

> שמות מ' פסוק ל"ח
> כי ענן ד' על המשכן יומם ואש תהיה לילה בו לעיני כל בית ישראל בכל מסעיהם:
>
> For the cloud of Hashem was on the Mishkan by day, and a fire would be on it by night, before the eyes of all Yisrael in all their travels.

The entire *Chumash* ends with this thought, that all was done before their own eyes:

> דברים ל"ד פסוק י"א - י"ב
> לכל האתת והמופתים אשר שלחו ד' לעשות בארץ מצרים לפרעה ולכל עבדיו ולכל ארצו: ולכל היד החזקה ולכל המורא הגדול אשר עשה משה לעיני כל ישראל:
>
> For all the signs and wonders which Hashem sent him to do in the land of Egypt, to Pharoah, all his servants and all his land. And for all the strong hand and all the great awesomeness which Moshe did to the eyes of all Yisrael.

The Torah made it clear in advance that *matan Torah* would be a national public occurrence:

> שמות י"ט פסוק ט
> ויאמר ד' אל משה הנה אנכי בא אליך בעב הענן בעבור ישמע העם בדברי עמך וגם בך יאמינו לעולם:
>
> Hashem said to Moshe, "Behold, I come to you in the thickness of the cloud in order that the people shall hear when I speak to you, and will also believe in you forever."

> שמות י"ט פסוק י"א
> והיו נכנים ליום השלישי כי ביום השלישי ירד ד' לעיני כל העם על הר סיני:
>
> They shall be ready for the third day, for on the third day Hashem will come down on Har Sinai before the eyes of all the people.

When the Torah relates the story of *matan Torah*, it emphasizes that they all saw:

> שמות כ' פסוק יד
>
> וכל העם ראים את הקולת ואת הלפידם ואת קול השפר ואת ההר עשן וירא העם וינעו ויעמדו מרחק:
>
> And all the people saw the thunder, the lightning, the sound of the shofar and the mountain smoking. The people saw and trembled, and stood from afar.

When Moshe Rabbeinu repeated the story of *matan Torah*, he reminded them that they all saw it personally:

> דברים ה' פסוק ד
>
> פנים בפנים דבר ד' עמכם בהר מתוך האש:
>
> Face to face Hashem spoke to you on the mountain from the midst of the fire.

Bnei Yisrael asked Moshe Rabbeinu to bring them the rest of the messages, instead of hearing them directly from Hashem, as they had the first time:

> דברים ה' פסוק כ"א-כ"ב
>
> ותאמרו הן הראנו ד' אלקינו את כבדו ואת גדלו ואת קלו שמענו מתוך האש היום הזה ראינו כי ידבר אלקים את האדם וחי: ועתה למה נמות כי תאכלנו האש הגדלה הזאת אם יספים אנחנו לשמע את קול ד' אלקינו עוד ומתנו:
>
> And you said, "Behold! Hashem, our G-d, has shown us His glory and His greatness. We heard His voice from inside the fire. Today we have seen that Hashem can speak to a man and he will (still) live. So, now, why should we die when this great fire will consume us? If we continue to hear the voice of Hashem, our G-d, we will die.

NO ONE ELSE BUT YOU

Moshe Rabbeinu reminds the Jewish people that they went through experiences by *matan Torah* and *yetzias Mitzrayim* that no one else ever did, nor will they ever even claim so:

> **דברים ד' פסוק לב- לה**
>
> כי שאל נא לימים ראשנים אשר היו לפניך למן היום אשר ברא אלקים אדם על הארץ ולמקצה השמים ועד קצה השמים הנהיה כדבר הגדול הזה או הנשמע כמהו: השמע עם קול אלקים מדבר מתוך האש כאשר שמעת אתה ויחי: או הנסה אלקים לבוא לקחת לו גוי מקרב גוי במסת באתת ובמופתים ובמלחמה וביד חזקה ובזרוע נטויה ובמוראים גדלים ככל אשר עשה לכם ד' אלקיכם במצרים לעיניך: אתה הראת לדעת כי ד' הוא האלקים אין עוד מלבדו:
>
> *Ask, if you will, about the earliest days, from the day Hashem created man on the earth, and from one end of the heavens to the other end. Did such a great thing as this ever happen, or was such a thing ever heard? Did a nation hear the voice of Hashem speaking from the midst of the fire as you heard, and live? Or did Hashem ever make miracles to come and take a nation to Himself from among another nation, with miracles, signs, wonders, war, a strong Hand and an outstretched Arm, as Hashem, your G-d, did for you in Mitzrayim, before your eyes? You have been shown to know that Hashem is G-d; there is none other besides Him.*

What happened to us — Hashem's revelation to an entire nation — never happened to anyone else. Furthermore, no one else ever even claimed that such a thing occurred to them.

That is what is meant by the words, "Or was anything like it heard?" Did we ever even hear anyone else claim that they had a public revelation from the Creator? The other religions, *l'havdil*, claim that one person had a revelation or made miracles (which no one can trace and can't be proven). No one else has ever had the audacity to claim that the Creator spoke to their nation publicly. As we shall yet see, it's simply too big a lie to get away with.

NEVER FORGET WHAT YOU SAW BY HAR SINAI

Nothing could be more important than remembering what took place at Har Sinai. Our entire faith is based on this.

> **דברים ד' פסוק ט - יב**
>
> רק השמר לך ושמר נפשך מאד פן תשכח את הדברים אשר ראו עיניך ופן יסורו מלבבך כל ימי חייך והודעתם לבניך ולבני בניך: יום אשר עמדת לפני ד' אלקיך בחרב באמר ד' אלי הקהל לי את העם ואשמעם את דברי אשר ילמדון

> ליראה אתי כל הימים אשר הם חיים על האדמה ואת בניהם ילמדון: ותקרבון ותעמדון תחת ההר וההר בער באש עד לב השמים חשך ענן וערפל: וידבר ד' אליכם מתוך האש קול דברים אתם שמעים ותמונה אינכם ראים זולתי קול:
>
> *(After telling us to keep all the mitzvos:) Only guard yourself and your nefesh very much, lest you forget the things that your [own] eyes saw, and lest they are removed from your heart all the days of your life. Tell them to your children and your grandchildren. The day that you stood before Hashem your G-d in Chorev, when Hashem said to me, "Gather the people to Me and I will let them hear My words, that they may learn to fear Me all the days that they live on the earth and will teach their children. You came close and stood at the bottom of the mountain. The mountain was burning in fire till the very heart of the heaven among darkness, cloud and thick cloud. Hashem spoke to you from the midst of the fire. You heard the voice with the words, but you did not see any picture, only voice."*

RAMBAN: KNOW WHERE THE MITZVOS CAME FROM

As we have seen in the above *pesukim*, the Torah forewarns us in very strong language never to forget what we saw at Har Sinai, because our entire faith stands on this. On this *pasuk*, the Ramban tells us how fundamental is this idea that we heard Hashem Yisborach speak to us directly, and that we must transmit this to our descendants in all future generations:

> **רמב"ן דברים פרק ד פסוק ט**
>
> רק השמר לך וגו' פן תשכח את הדברים. וכו' הכתוב הזה לפי דעתי מצות לא תעשה הזהיר בה מאד כי כאשר אמר שנזהר בכל המצוות ונשמור החוקים והמשפטים לעשותם חזר ואמר רק אני מזהירך מאד להשמר ולשמור עצמך מאד מאד לזכור מאין באו אליך המצות שלא תשכח מעמד הר סיני מכל הדברים אשר ראו שם עיניך הקולות והלפידים את כבודו ואת גדלו ודבריו אשר שמעת שם מתוך האש ותודיע כל הדברים אשר ראו עיניך במעמד הנכבד ההוא לבניך ולבני בניך עד עולם:
>
> *"Only guard yourself, etc., lest you forget the things, etc."*
>
> *This verse, according to my understanding, is a negative command. Here the Torah forewarns us very much. After Moshe Rabbeinu said how careful we must be to fulfill the mitzvos and keep all the chukim and mishpatim, he follows up by saying,*

> But I forewarn you very much to be guarded and to guard yourself very, very much to remember from where these mitzvos came to you. That you should never forget the Revelation at Har Sinai; all the things that your eyes saw there; the thunder and the lightning; His glory and greatness, and His words that you heard from the midst of the fire. You should inform your children and your grandchildren forever of all the things that your eyes saw at that significant event.

Ramban continues:

> ופירש הטעם כי השם עשה המעמד ההוא כדי שתלמדו ליראה אותו כל הימים ואת בניכם תלמדון לדורות עולם אם כן עשו אתם ככה ואל תשכחו אותו: והנה קודם שיזכיר הדברות שנאמרו שם הזהיר במצות לא תעשה שלא נשכח דבר מן המעמד ההוא ולא נסירהו מלבנו לעולם וצוה במצות עשה שנודיע בו לכל זרענו מדור לדור כל מה שהיה שם בראיה ובשמיעה
>
> And he explains the reason (you must never forget): Because Hashem made that event in order that you should fear Him all the days, and you shall teach your children for all generations, eternally. If so, do it (indeed) and don't forget it. Behold, now, before He reminds them of the (ten) commandments which were said there, He forewarns them with a negative command not to forget anything from that occurrence and forever not to remove it from our heart. He commanded us with a positive commandment to inform all our posterity from generation to generation about all that we saw and heard there.

Ramban continues:

> והתועלת במצוה הזאת גדולה מאד שאם היו דברי התורה באים אלינו מפי משה בלבד אע"פ שנבואתו נתאמתה באותות ובמופתים אם יקום בקרבנו נביא או חולם חלום ויצונו בהפך מן התורה ונתן אלינו אות או מופת יכנס ספק בלב האנשים אבל כשהגיע אלינו התורה מפי הגבורה לאזנינו ועינינו הרואות אין שם אמצעי, נכחיש כל חולק וכל מספק, ונשקר אותו, לא יועילהו אות ולא יצילהו מופת מן המיתה בידינו כי אנחנו היודעים בשקרותו:
>
> The benefit of this mitzvah is very great. If the words of the Torah were coming to us solely from Moshe's words, even though we were convinced of his prophecy through signs and wonders, if a prophet or a dreamer of dreams would arise among us and command us the opposite (of the Torah), and give us a sign or a wonder, a doubt might enter people's hearts. But

> since the Torah came to our ears from the Almighty Himself, and our eyes saw with no go-between, we will contradict anyone who argues or makes doubts. We will declare him a liar. His sign will not help him and his wonder will not save him from death by our hands, because we know that he is lying.

Ramban continues:

> זהו שאמר שם (שמות יט ט) וגם בך יאמינו לעולם כי בשנעתיק גם כן הדבר לבנינו ידעו שהיה הדבר אמת בלא ספק כאלו ראוהו כל הדורות כי לא נעיד שקר לבנינו ולא ננחיל אותם דבר הבל ואין בם מועיל. והם לא יסתפקו כלל בעדותנו שנעיד להם אבל יאמינו בודאי שראינו כולנו בעינינו וכל מה שספרנו להם.

> That is what the pasuk says there, "And they will also believe in You forever." Because, when we will give this over to our children, they will know that this thing is true without a doubt as if all the generations had seen all this (themselves), for (they know) that we will not testify a lie to our children, nor give them a worthless heritage of no benefit. They won't have any doubts about our testimony that we tell them, but rather they will surely believe that we all saw this with our eyes, and believe everything that we tell them.

Ramban has told us in no uncertain terms how absolutely vital it is to know that we ourselves were the witnesses to all that transpired. This is the most fundamental principle of our *emunah*.

RAMBAM: THE ULTIMATE BELIEF

The Rambam, as well, states clearly that the foundation of our belief in Moshe Rabbeinu and the Torah is that we heard Hashem appoint Moshe to be His prophet.

> רמב"ם הלכות יסודי התורה פרק ח הלכה א
> משה רבינו לא האמינו בו ישראל מפני האותות שעשה, שהמאמין על פי האותות יש בלבו דופי שאפשר שיעשה האות בלט וכשוף אלא כל האותות שעשה משה במדבר לפי הצורך עשאם לא להביא ראיה על הנבואה וכו'. ובמה האמינו בו במעמד הר סיני שעינינו ראו ולא זר ואזנינו שמעו ולא אחר האש והקולות והלפידים והוא נגש אל הערפל והקול מדבר אליו ואנו שומעים "משה משה לך אמור להן כך וכך......."

> *The Jewish people did not believe in Moshe Rabbeinu because of the signs which he made. A person who believes based on signs can always have in his heart some doubt. Perhaps the sign was made through magic. Rather, all the signs that Moshe made were for a specific purpose, not to bring a proof about his prophecy... When did we believe in him? By ma'amad Har Sinai, where our own eyes saw, not a stranger's. Our own ears heard, not someone else's, the thunder and the lightning. Moshe approached the cloud. We heard, "Moshe, Moshe. Go and say to them such and such......"*

By now, it should be very clear that this is indeed the Torah's claim, which the Jewish people have reiterated ever since we became a nation: that we personally saw and experienced all the miraculous happenings from the time Moshe Rabbeinu arrived in Mitzrayim, until (at least) the end of the forty years in the desert.

CHAPTER FIVE

Our Claim Is Indeed True

Unless it really all happened as we claim it did, how is it possible that an entire people came to accept this belief unanimously, continued believing in it wherever they lived, and passed it on to their children in an unbroken chain down to this very day? They adhered to the dictates of this Torah unswervingly. Throughout the ages, Jews were so convinced of its truth that they were almost always willing to give their lives for it. How did they come to believe that all these things happened to them? A nonbeliever needs to answer this fundamental question. In order for an intellectually honest skeptic to reject belief in our claim, there seem to be only two options: that the Torah was written by Moshe, or that the Torah was written by another person (or group of people) at some later time.

THE MOSHE OPTION

The first possibility is to admit that there really was a person named Moshe, who gave a Torah to that first generation. However, the skeptic may say, Moshe lied to the Jewish people. He told them that the Torah was given to him by G-d, but in fact he had made it up himself. Moshe was a great orator, possessed of great charisma. He dazzled the people with his brilliance (or had an army that forced them to accept his Torah).

THE CHAIM YANKEL OPTION

A second alternative for the skeptic is to claim something like this: The Torah was introduced at some later point by someone else, we know not who. (We'll call him Chaim Yankel, arbitrarily). Chaim Yankel came along (somewhere, sometime, we don't really know) and told the people that G-d appeared to him and gave him this Torah. Actually, Chaim Yankel explained, the people had been given the Torah much earlier in history, but because they were wicked and disobeyed it, it had fallen into disuse and been forgotten. (Alternatively, because of various historical upheavals such as war and exile, the Torah had been forgotten.) Now G-d had told him to remind the people of what they once had been given, long ago at the time of (the fictitious) Moshe Rabbeinu. Alternatively, Chaim Yankel said he was digging in his backyard and discovered this ancient scroll, which had apparently been forgotten by the Jewish people. He told them that now they must return to their national heritage as found in the newly discovered scroll. Eventually, the Jews set about keeping all six hundred and thirteen mitzvos.

These seem to be the only two possible scenarios that a skeptic could rely on to explain how the Jewish people accepted the Torah and believed in it so fervently.

NEITHER OPTION WILL WORK

When you think about it, though, neither option makes sense. Let's pursue option number one. The skeptic says that Moshe pulled the wool over the eyes of the people (or maybe was hallucinating). He packed a large knapsack with food and sneaked up to Har Sinai, where he camped out for forty days. When he returned, he claimed that G-d had given him a Torah, which they were to begin keeping immediately. No nonsense allowed, or G-d will bring His wrath on the people. The people believed him and began keeping the Torah.

Before we proceed, a short but vital introduction: Rav Yehuda Halevi in his classic work *Kuzari* tells us a fundamental principle — you cannot convince people that they had experiences they know they never had. Gullible people may accept the silliest ideas and believe that others had those experiences, but they will simply never believe you when you tell them they had the experiences. They know it's nothing but a big lie, because these things never happened to them.

If Moshe had made wild claims, the people would surely have asked for some substantiation. As far back as anyone can remember, Jews are not pushovers. We try to buy wholesale and haggle over the price! We can assume that our ancestors were similar in nature, but even if they were naive, it is difficult to imagine that they would have just have accepted six hundred and thirteen new, complicated and restrictive mitzvos on the spur of the moment. The Jews of the time would have demanded lots of proof and a solid basis before complying. Even if Moshe performed miracles upon miracles for them, they still would have demanded to see this Torah which Moshe claimed was given to him by G-d. One look in the Torah would have told them that it is false. Why would they know that the Torah is false?

Remember that the Torah makes it crystal clear throughout that it was presented to the first generation, who saw everything with their own eyes. In this option, the people receiving this Torah are supposed to be that first generation. They could never have accepted it, because it would have been obvious to them that it was a lie from beginning to end. It states that they had seen and experienced things which they knew they never saw and never experienced. Even the least intelligent and most gullible of people could never accept such silliness. They would have asked Moshe some pretty tough questions:

- It says here in your Torah that the waters of the Red Sea stood up in two walls on either side of us, while we walked through. You know that never happened. We were chased to the Sea, took off our socks, waded across at low tide, and luckily the high tide caught the Egyptians off-guard and they all drowned.
- You say here that we eat food that falls from the sky every day, six days a week, with a double portion on Friday. You know very well that we never saw such a silly thing. No bread ever fell from the sky. We go out in the desert searching for wild plants and berries.

- You say that we have a stone that travels with us, and when you hit it, it gives enough water for the entire people. This is a lie. We know of no such thing. We go out searching for cactus water or any other water we can find.
- You say that we all saw the mountain tremble, the thunder and the lightning. Then we experienced prophecy by the Ten Commandments when G-d spoke to you and to us together. This is a lie. We heard and saw nothing of the kind. You went up to the mountain for the forty days, we waited for you, and you came back with this Torah of yours. You said that G-d had given it to you.

Everything you have written here is totally false.

Even if the Torah made no demands on them, they would have rejected it. Certainly they could never have accepted a Torah which demands so very much, when it is obviously false. Since the Jewish people in Moshe's generation did accept the Torah and keep the commandments, it can only be because they recognized it as being completely true. They indeed experienced all those marvelous things, and didn't need to be forced or convinced. Furthermore it is hard to imagine why any forger in his right mind would write a false Torah that immediately arouses so many unanswerable questions. It's pretty obvious that option one simply could never have happened. The Jewish people never could have accepted and believed major, central events in their lives that never happened, and never would have accepted significant limitations to their lives when they knew very well that the whole book was not true.

WHO HAD THE REVELATION?

Let's demonstrate these thoughts with a down-to-earth illustration. Imagine, if you will, that tomorrow I go downtown to one of the busiest street corners in the city. I build myself a modest platform and soon a small crowd starts to gather. I then ascend to the top with a megaphone and proclaim, "Hear ye, hear ye! I had a revelation last night."

Curiosity seekers begin to gather around, and now I have quite a crowd of listeners. I speak very dramatically.

"Last night I was lying on my bed, unable to sleep. There was a full moon and the stars were shining. Suddenly, a heavenly face peered in at me through my third-story window. The face was kind and full of love. Never in my life had I seen anything like it before. At last, the Being spoke, in a voice full of pity and compassion. 'Know that I am the Master of the Universe. I have come to redeem mankind from the evils of society. You, George Kedidelhoffer, are to be my prophet and my messenger. You will proclaim my word throughout the world by forming a group called the Redeemers of the Universe. Through this group you shall change the face of all mankind. Sickness and poverty, war and violence shall all disappear.' These were the words of the Master of the Universe, exactly as he spoke them to me last night."

By the time I have finished, perspiration is running down my face. Deep emotion is reflected in my face. I am obviously sincere in everything I have said. I urge the people to rally around the banner of the new sect I intend to create, so that we can redeem mankind from the ailments of society.

Would there be simpletons among the crowd who will be fooled by my charisma, emotion and eloquence? There certainly could be some. They might tell their friends about me, and the movement might catch on. If the Reverend Moon[11] could do it, so can I. Right?

The point is that there are many gullible people in the world. These people have no way of knowing whether I am telling them the truth or not.[12] Just as there are no witnesses to say that I did have the claimed revelation, there can be no witnesses to contradict this claim. My listeners will pass judgment on me based solely on how profound an impression I have made on them. If they think I am sincere and they are infatuated with my charming personality, they may walk away feeling that I have told them the truth. If, in addition, I am telling them things that they want to hear (for example, how the world is going to improve

---

11 A highly successful cult leader, whose followers believed him to be the Messiah. This cult has thousands of followers and owns extensive properties around the globe.

12 The Maharal of Prague (*Tiferes Yisroel*, p. 177) teaches us a fundamental principle. "He who wishes to lie testifies about far-off matters." Charlatans will never speak of things which the populace can easily check out, for then their bluff will be called. Instead, they weave their false tales about matters which the people know nothing about. Then, if they are convincing, the people will accept their claims out of sheer ignorance.

and how all their problems will soon disappear), they are all the more enticed to accept me. Not everyone, of course, but certainly the simplest element of the population can easily be taken in by such a hoax. Then it might spread.

Those who reject the beliefs of the Jewish nation by choosing option one are actually suggesting that something along these lines happened to us. We, too, were taken in by such a charlatan some time long ago, and began believing that we had been told the truth.

We maintain that this is not only false, but rather downright nonsensical. Whoever introduced the Torah to us could not have told us, "I had a revelation." He really must have said, "You had a revelation."

YOU HAD A REVELATION!

If the Torah were a hoax, it would have to be compared to a different, although similar, scenario. Instead of telling the people that I had a revelation, let's suppose I tell them that they had a revelation.

"You were lying on your bed last night. You saw the heavenly face, etc." Will anyone believe me? Even the simplest, most gullible element in the crowd will turn their backs on the raving lunatic. Although some people can be tricked into believing that I had a supernatural experience, they definitely cannot be made to think that they have had experiences I've fabricated out of thin air. After all, they know that they experienced no such revelation.

In light of the fact that the Jewish people have always claimed to have witnessed all the miracles and experienced the Revelation personally, a skeptic (who chooses option one) would have to contend that whoever sold our forefathers this bill of goods was somehow able to convince them that they themselves had heard G-d speak to them. Not only that, but also that every single man, woman and child saw the water of the Red Sea pile up into two walls, through which the people passed in safety on dry land. He convinced them that they had eaten bread which fell from the sky every day, wherever they encamped. This lasted for forty years straight. The bread fell only six days a week. Of course, no manna fell on Shabbos. What did they eat on Shabbos? What a silly question! A double portion of manna fell every Friday. This didn't happen to cousin Charlie, Aunt Tilly or the guy down the street. It happened to each and every one of them. Quite a feat, indeed! (Even in option two, he would have to convince them that all of these never-heard-of-before experiences happened to all their ancestors.) This impostor was some salesman!

This is what the Torah repeatedly says: The generation that first received the Torah was the very same generation that experienced the ten plagues, the splitting of the Red Sea and all the other miracles, along with the subsequent Revelation. G-d spoke to the people who saw all these things themselves. He gave His Torah to the people who personally experienced all the "proof" of its authenticity. Their information was based not on hearsay, but on eyewitness testimony.

The position of all the competing religions (as we shall soon see), is that of "I had a revelation." Our position is clearly that of "You had a revelation."

It seems quite obvious that no one would actually contend that our people had been duped in this fashion. Yet, in order for one to remain skeptical of our historical tradition, this is the stance which he must take, unless he chooses option two. Option two, as we will see, is not any more sensible than option one.

CHAPTER SIX

Well, Maybe It Happened Differently

Now for option two. The skeptic will propose the other scenario. Here he is going to run into trouble. This suggestion is just as ridiculous as the first. If there never was a Moshe Rabbeinu, and the Torah was presented some time later in history by some impostor (Chaim Yankel) who claimed that the Torah had somehow been lost but was now revealed to him by G-d, or which he found by digging near his tent, he would have had to answer some serious questions:

This Torah says that all these miraculous things happened to our ancestors, who numbered a few million. How is it possible that not the slightest echo of this ever filtered down to any of the people until you, Chaim Yankel, came along? How could the *makkos, krias Yam Suf,* the *mann,* the Revelation, etc., all be totally obliterated from the public memory? How could it be that our entire people once had a Torah, believed in it and kept its commandments, but we have no recollection whatsoever that it ever existed?

Furthermore, in this Torah you present us it says that the Torah will never be forgotten. How can you tell us that it has become so forgotten that nobody ever heard of it.

> **דברים לא פסוק כא**
>
> והיה כי תמצאן אתו רעות רבות וצרות וענתה השירה הזאת לפניו לעד כי לא תשכח מפי זרעו.
>
> *It will come to pass when many terrible tragic things befall them, this song (Ha'azinu) will speak up before them as a witness, for it shall never be forgotten from the mouths of their children.*

In addition, we can ask: Is it possible that an entire nation should accept a Torah such as this overnight, with so many endless dos and don'ts, without putting up a massive fuss? The same way that our modern day skeptic struggles with belief, they certainly would have struggled all the more so then, because they knew that up till that day no one had ever heard of a Torah. If indeed they resisted, it must have taken a massive effort and lots of time to either coerce them or convince them. How come there is no historical memory of this struggle?

WHO AND WHERE IS THE MISSING HERO?

How is it possible that the memory of this impostor has been totally lost? We don't know when or where or how this happened. Did he hypnotize them to begin believing that they had always had the Torah and handed it down from the first generation? We know of the origins of every other religion, who founded them, when and where. Yet, if this is the origin of the Jewish belief, there should be some memory that up until a certain time the people had no Torah, but then Chaim Yankel revealed it to them and they started keeping it. After all, the Bible is probably the most widely circulated book in history. It introduced morality to the world, and is considered sacred by millions and millions. Shouldn't there be some memory of how it came to be or who introduced it to the world?

WE ARE CONFIDENT

The *mesorah* of *Am Yisrael* is ironclad. As far as our people have always been concerned,[13] the Revelation at Sinai and all the other miraculous

---

13   This was true until the advent of Reform two hundred years ago.

events have been testified to by millions of witnesses. They are our ancestors, who witnessed everything with their own eyes and transmitted it all to their children throughout the generations. The Pesach Seder has always been an opportunity to transmit this tradition. We recently celebrated the Pesach Seder for the three thousand, three hundred and twenty-seventh time! The first time it was performed was in Mitzrayim the night before the Exodus. We have never stopped making a Seder ever since. The Exodus has been a running theme throughout our daily lives for thousands of years.

We all know how argumentative Jews are and have been as long as we have recorded history. Put three Jews in one room and you wind up with four opinions! Despite this historic tendency to argue on everything and everyone, this traditional "version" of our origin was unanimously accepted by Jews all over the world. In communities across Europe and in all the Sephardic lands, this was the only story of our history. Only Jews who adopted a new lifestyle, such as the Hellenists, rejected the national history in order to accommodate their new mode of life. They had no new evidence and certainly no historical tradition to back up their heresy, only their desire that it be so. Until the advent of Reform (at the end of the seventeen hundreds), the vast majority of Jewish communities everywhere believed fervently in the historicity of the miracles of the Exodus and *ma'amad Har Sinai*. Even the *Tzedukim* and the *Kara'im* didn't dispute that. Christianity also agrees fully that there was a Revelation. Their only issue is their claim that later on G-d changed his mind and chose them instead of us. Islam believes in a Revelation, but claims we distorted the Bible to contradict Islam.[14] Josephus, a Jewish historian of two thousand years ago, speaks about our people believing this unanimously, and feeling as if Moshe Rabbeinu is still looking over their shoulder.

The *nevi'im* rebuked the people for every type of sin imaginable, except for one. Never is there a mention of someone that didn't believe in the

---

14　This is a ridiculous contention. The *Sefer Torah* had been in existence for seventeen hundred years, and the Greek translation was already in the hands of the gentiles some eight hundred years before the advent of Islam.

Exodus or the Revelation. This is in sharp contrast to the Christian Bible, which hurls threats and curses on all those who didn't believe in their "Savior." The Quran as well threatens and curses all those who do not accept Mohammed's new religion, which was spread either by some people believing in Mohammed's private revelation, or else by the sword of Mohammed's armies that conquered many nations. Each of these systems condemns all nonbelievers to eternal Hell.

The Jewish people didn't need to be convinced, threatened or coerced. They knew that it was all true. Moshe Rabbeinu tells them numerous times that there can be no justification for not keeping it, because they know it's all true.

CHAPTER SEVEN

What Could the Motive Be?

According to the skeptic, the Torah is a forgery. Whoever wrote it intended to give the impression that it was given by G-d, when actually he invented the whole thing. Whenever something is forged, there is always a motive for the forgery. A fake signature on a check is for the purpose of stealing money. When an impostor tries to pretend he is someone other than he really is, there is always some ulterior motive.

If, as the skeptic proposes, the Torah is such a forgery, then the perpetrator would have wanted to gain something for himself. If it was money he was after, he would have allotted himself or his family some special position with a hefty salary. If it was power, he would have made himself a dictator whose every word would be law. After all, he's making it all up to suit himself. The problem is that there doesn't seem to be any motive that the skeptic could attribute to his imagined forger.

"Well," the skeptic might say, "Moshe Rabbeinu was the mastermind who wrote the Torah. He established his authority as the leader by claiming that G-d chose him to be the prophet." Isn't it strange, then, that no salary is allotted to Moshe, no stipulation that his children will inherit his position, and no mention of any authoritative powers? Indeed, Yehoshua took over after him, not Moshe's children. Also, would Moshe have written that at the end of his career, he sinned and was punished by G-d?

"Perhaps it was the *Kohanim* or the *Levi'im*." Would the *Kohanim* have written that it was Aharon who was held responsible for making the golden calf? Would the *Levi'im* have penned the disgraceful story of Levi participating in the massacre of Shechem? Neither of these groups is allotted a very exorbitant salary for their respective services. The *Kohanim* receive the *terumah*, which is a small allotment from the grain harvest of the other tribes. In addition they get to eat the meat of sacrifices and a few other small items from the Temple service. No bonuses, no paid vacations, no expense accounts! The *Levi'im* get the *ma'aser*, which is ten percent of the grain, oil and wine which the nation produces. However, neither they nor the *Kohanim* received any land whatsoever. The other tribes all got a portion of Eretz Yisrael, but they did not. At best, their income approaches that of the rest. The *Levi* didn't get this in a paycheck. He had to go around collecting it from the farmers by their silos. The *pasuk* makes this crystal clear in reference to both *Kohanim* and *Levi'im*.

> **במדבר פרק יח פסוק ב**
>
> ויאמר ד' אל אהרן בארצם לא תנחל וחלק לא יהיה לך בתוכם אני חלקך ונחלתך בתוך בני ישראל:
>
> *Hashem said to Aharon, "In their land you shall not inherit, and no share shall you have among them. I am your share and your inheritance among Bnei Yisrael."*

> **במדבר פרק יח פסוק כג - כד**
>
> ועבד הלוי הוא את עבדת אהל מועד והם ישאו עונם חקת עולם לדרתיכם ובתוך בני ישראל לא ינחלו נחלה: כי את מעשר בני ישראל אשר ירימו לד' תרומה נתתי ללוים לנחלה על כן אמרתי להם בתוך בני ישראל לא ינחלו נחלה:
>
> *He, the Levi, shall perform the service of the Ohel Mo'ed, and they (the Levi'im) shall bear their sins (of non-Levi'im who approach to perform the*

> Levi'im's jobs). It is an everlasting law for all your generations. For it is the tithe of Bnei Yisrael, which they will separate for Hashem, that I have given the Levi'im for an inheritance. Among the Bnei Yisrael they will not receive any inheritance.

Perhaps it was the Rabbis who made up the Torah in order to boss the people around, by making laws and setting themselves up as the ultimate authority. However, this can't be: the position of Rabbi is never mentioned anywhere in the Torah. The *shoftim* (judges) are indeed mentioned numerous times, but without reference to any special benefits, honors or power. Here, too, there is no allotment of salary. Nor is it specified who the judges will be. Why would a faker create a position without somehow indicating that he or his family will hold that position?

Every forgery has a forger. And every forger has a motive. It seems clear that there is no one to attribute a motive for falsifying the Torah.

WHO WOULD WRITE THIS?

The skeptic would like to dismiss the Torah as nothing less than a forgery. Someone, somewhere, sometime (we know not who, where or when) told the people some story about a G-d giving a Torah, they accepted it and began keeping its laws. We have already shown what a far-fetched contention this is. Here, we can add another point. If someone forged the Torah, how long would they want their trick to last? Would a forger write things that would make the people realize its falsehood almost immediately? Here are a few examples to consider:

The Torah commands us to keep the *shemittah* every seventh year. No work is to be done on the fields (except what is necessary to keep the trees alive). No crops for an entire year! Let us grant, for argument's sake, that this impostor wanted to impose this command on the people. How will the people manage for an entire year with no grain or produce? How will they support themselves with no income for a year? The one who is bringing the Torah to the people and claiming it is full of Hashem's absolute rules for life, must have a response to this question. The people he is trying to fool are surely going to ask him this basic question! What would be the most sensible answer for the impostor to offer? He would probably say that the people should store away part of their crop during the first six years of the cycle, so that they won't starve during the seventh year. But no! The Torah's answer to the question is very different: Don't worry! G-d will give you a double crop during the sixth year, enough to last you until the next crop comes in after the Sabbatical year. I promise! A forger would have to be an idiot to write such a thing! After the first cycle, when no double crop came during the sixth year, the nation will know that the book was not in fact given by G-d.

> ויקרא פרק כה פסוק כ
> וכי תאמרו מה נאכל בשנה השביעת הן לא נזרע ולא נאסף את תבואתנו: וצויתי את ברכתי לכם בשנה הששית ועשת את התבואה לשלש השנים:
>
> *And if you will say, "What will we eat in the seventh year? Behold! We don't plant and we don't gather in our grain." I will command my blessing to you in the sixth year, and it will make grain for the three years (sixth, seventh, and eighth until crop comes).*

Likewise, the Torah prescribed a pilgrimage to the Beis Hamikdash three times a year. All the males are obligated to go. (It is likely that many or most of the women and children went, too.) How long will it take before the surrounding nations hear that the cities are left defenseless three times a year? Surely they will come and plunder everything of value and massacre anyone they find who stayed behind. The person presenting a Torah, or claiming that he has found the long-lost Torah, will surely be asked this question. One would expect him to say that the men should take turns staying home to guard the city. Every festival, a different group will take its turn. Nothing of the sort! His response: There is nothing to worry about. I promise that no one will covet your land when you go up to the Temple three times a year. It's pretty hard to imagine anyone wanting to pull off a hoax of this magnitude giving such ridiculous answers!

> **שמות פרק לד פסוק כג-כד**
>
> שלש פעמים בשנה יראה כל זכורך את פני האדן ד' אלקי ישראל: כי אוריש גוים מפניך והרחבתי את גבלך ולא יחמד איש את ארצך בעלתך לראות את פני ד' אלקיך שלש פעמים בשנה:
>
> *Three times a year all your males shall appear before the Master, Hashem, the G-d of Israel. For I will chase out nations from before you, and I will widen your border. No man will covet your land when you go up to appear before Hashem, your G-d, three times a year.*

CHAPTER EIGHT

Other Beliefs: Unproved and Unprovable

THE CLAIMS OF OTHERS

*P*erhaps our claim, although significant, may not be so impressive because other faiths make similar claims. When everyone makes similar claims, we tend to become skeptical of all of them. Imagine that we are at a jeweler's trade show. Each vendor claims that his diamonds are of the highest quality, but that his competitor's diamonds are fake. Perhaps all of them are lying. But what if we take out a loupe (the special magnifier that jewelers use to study jewels), and we see clearly that one vendor's diamonds are genuine while the others' are indeed fake? Then we realize that the vendor of the genuine merchandise was the only one really telling the truth.

In matters of *emunah*, we need to "take out the loupe" and examine the evidence very carefully. Once we do so, it will be clear that there is absolutely no comparison at all between our claim and the claims of others.

All other beliefs, if they claim to believe in G-d (such as Christianity and Islam), are based on the word of a single individual.

ISLAM

Mohammed said that the angel Gavriel appointed him to start a new religion and became the chosen prophet of Allah during a private revelation in a cave. Who was present to witness this revelation?[15]

Mohammed gained most of his followers by threatening them with his sword. He sent out armies across the Middle East and conquered many nations. They gave up their idol worship and adopted Islam. This is not merely what we say about them. Rather, this is their own version of how their religion started. If Mohammed were here today and told you his story, you would undoubtedly say, "Prove it!" No substantiation or proof has ever been forthcoming in the last fourteen hundred years. The Quran is full of threats and curses on anyone not believing in Islam. Obviously, many didn't believe, because there was no substantiation whatsoever.

CHRISTIANITY

Christianity was originally a Jewish sect. Most Jews had no interest in it. Even the Christian Bible (which they call the New Testament) makes it clear that most of the Nazarene's disciples and followers were illiterates, from the lowest segments of society. The Nazarene (Jesus) was a Jew, and he remained a Jew throughout all his life. Although he broke some laws, he basically kept most of the mitzvos. He stated clearly that he had not come to change one iota of the (Torah) law. Although he didn't live up to his words, he was nevertheless a Jew. Shortly after Jesus' death, his disciples began to preach that their religion was for everyone, including

---

15 According to Islam, Mohammed's first revelation was the event in which Mohammed was visited by the archangel Gabriel who revealed to him a verse from the Quran. The event took place in a cave called Hira, located on the mountain called Jabal-an-Nour, near Mecca. According to biographies of Mohammed, the archangel Gabriel appears to him and commands him to recite the first lines of chapter 96 of the Quran. Mohammed's experience is mentioned in the Quran 53:4-9. (Wikipedia)

Other Beliefs: Unproved and Unprovable

non-Jews. Sometime later, along came a Jew named Shaul of Tarshish, whose main talent was as a salesman. (He later changed his name to Paul.) It was mainly through his efforts that Christianity spread among gentiles. He realized that this new religion was not "selling" well among the Jews, so he decided to peddle it to the gentiles. Of course, the gentiles would not accept such a heavy responsibility of six hundred thirteen commandments, including circumcision. So Paul said that on one of his trips he had a revelation from Jesus, who commissioned him to bring the new religion to the gentiles. Paul repeatedly states that the Torah has been retracted. Circumcision is no longer necessary. From now on "salvation" is conditional on belief in the Nazarene.

Although most Christian sects advocate doing good deeds, in the end of it all, without faith in Jesus, no matter how much *teshuvah*, *tzedakah*, good deeds and mitzvos a person does, only hell awaits him. Some even say that with belief you will get paradise upon death, no matter what sins you have committed or how wicked a person you have been.[16] However, all agree that without signing on the dotted line, nothing will save you from the fires of the purgatory.

Now, honestly, if you were living in the time of Paul, don't you think you would have asked him some pretty tough questions? You would surely have asked, "On what basis should we believe you that the Torah

---

16 An interesting illustration of this classic Christian teaching: Eichmann was the Nazi official who was one of the main perpetrators of the Holocaust. He fled to Argentina and was eventually kidnapped by the Israeli government, flown to Israel to stand on trial, and condemned to be executed. During the Eichmann trial in Jerusalem, the Israeli government assigned the Reverend William Hall, a Canadian missionary who'd been living in Jerusalem for thirty years, as personal chaplain to Eichmann. Even in the face of his impending execution, Eichmann remained to the last an unrepentant Nazi. Under questioning, Rev. Hall stated that had Eichmann accepted his "Savior," he would have immediately entered the gates of Paradise without passing through purgatory at all. "Even though he had a hand in the murder of six million Jews?" Hall was asked. "Had Eichmann embraced the Church before his execution," Hall replied, "he would have been absolved of guilt and had a place in Paradise." "And what of the souls of his six million Jewish victims?" "They," Hall asserted, "would certainly not have entered Paradise; on the contrary, they were consigned to Hell because they had not accepted the Church's salvation." Some, it seems, have placed a policeman at Heaven's gates. Chaim Shapiro, *Once Upon a Shtetl* (Mesorah Publications, 1996), 255.

has been retracted and that from now on, all depends on belief in Jesus? After all, Hashem gave it openly and publicly to a few million Jews. Don't you think that if G-d wanted to retract His Torah that he should have informed us about it, so that we don't have to burn in Hell forever? Would it have been difficult for him to gather the people once again to Mount Sinai or some other place, and tell us that He'd had a change of heart? Furthermore, does G-d really change His mind? Doesn't the Torah tell us numerous times that it is forever and ever?[17] This thought is expressed in the commentary of the Malbim:

> מלבי"ם שמות יט פסוק ט
>
> רצה ד' שתנתן התורה בפרסום גדול ובריבוי עצום של ששים ריבוא (רק הגברים) והם הנחילו הקבלה הזאת אשר ראו בעיניהם לבניהם אחריהם לדור אחרון. ועל כן כל מי שיקום לאמור שהוא שליח מן ד' ליתן תורה לעם נשיב אליו תורה שלא תנתן מאת האלקים בפרסום גדול כזה אינה אלקית וכל שכן שלא לבטל התורה הנתונה ממשה שישיבו לו שצריך שיתראה ד' בעצמו לפני ששים ריבוא בפרסום גדול כמו שהתגלה בעת נתינתה כי בדבר המצווה לנביא בינו לבין עצמו יש חשש וספק בדבריו אפילו בדורו וכל שכן בדורות אחרים.
>
> *Hashem wanted the Torah to be given in a great public manner, in front of a vast amount of people, six hundred thousand men (besides women and children). They gave over this tradition that they had seen with their own eyes to their children, down to the last generation. Therefore, anyone who will arise to say that he is a messenger from Hashem to give a Torah to the people, we will say to him that a Torah which is not given in as public a manner as this is not from G-d. Certainly (we will not believe him) to nullify the Torah which was given by Moshe. We will tell him that (in order to retract it) Hashem needs to appear personally in front of six hundred thousand, just as He revealed Himself at the time that it was given. Anything (supposedly) commanded to a prophet in private is subject to suspicion and doubt even in his generation, certainly in other generations.*

The people who originally accepted Christianity were ignorant of the Torah, and were taken in by Paul's salesmanship. He told them he had a

---

17 There are many other valid reasons for rejecting both Christianity and Islam, but here we focus only on their lack of any historical basis.

revelation. Some didn't believe, of course, but those who did accepted it as fact and passed it on to their children. But what basis does this have?

Compare this with our claim. If you had been there, there would have been no need to convince you, since you saw everything yourself.

As mentioned above, the Rambam also makes the point that everyone saw. He continues:

> רמב"ם הלכות יסודי התורה פרק ח הלכה ב
>
> נמצאו אלו ששולח להן הם העדים על נבואתו שהיא אמת ואינו צריך לעשות להן אות אחר, שהם והוא עדים בדבר כשני עדים שראו דבר אחד ביחד שכל אחד מהן עד לחבירו שהוא אומר אמת ואין אחד מהן צריך להביא ראיה לחבירו, כך משה רבינו כל ישראל עדים לו אחר מעמד הר סיני ואינו צריך לעשות להם אות.
>
> *The people to whom Moshe Rabbeinu was sent are the very witnesses that his prophecy is true, and he doesn't need to make any other sign for them. They and he are the witnesses to this matter, just as two witnesses that saw something together. Each one knows that his fellow witness is testifying truthfully and neither of them needs any proof to verify his fellow witness' testimony. So, too, with Moshe Rabbeinu. All Yisrael are witnesses for him after ma'amad Har Sinai, and no further sign is necessary.*

In the following passage, the Rambam's hidden agenda is to refute Christianity and Islam.

> שם הלכה ג
>
> לפיכך אם עמד הנביא ועשה אותות ומופתים גדולים ובקש להכחיש נבואתו של משה רבינו אין שומעין לו ואנו יודעין בבאור שאותן האותות בלט וכשוף הן, לפי שנבואת משה רבינו אינה על פי האותות כדי שנערוך אותות זה לאותות זה, אלא בעינינו ראינוה ובאזנינו שמענוה כמו ששמע הוא, הא למה הדבר דומה לעדים שהעידו לאדם על דבר שראה בעיניו שאינו כמו שראה שאינו שומע להן אלא יודע בודאי שהן עדי שקר, לפיכך אמרה תורה שאם בא האות והמופת לא תשמע אל דברי הנביא ההוא, שהרי זה בא אליך באות ומופת להכחיש מה שראית בעיניך והואיל ואין אנו מאמינים במופת אלא מפני המצות שצונו משה היאך נקבל מאות זה שבא להכחיש נבואתו של משה שראינו וששמענו.
>
> *Therefore, if a prophet will arise and perform great signs and wonders, wanting to contradict the prophecy of Moshe Rabbeinu, we will not listen*

> to him. We will know with certainty that those signs were performed with magic. Because (our acceptance of) Moshe Rabbeinu's prophecy is not based on signs, so that we should measure the signs of one prophet against the signs of the other (to see whose are bigger). Rather, with our own eyes we saw it and with our own ears we heard it, just as he (Moshe Rabbeinu) himself heard it. To what can this be compared? To witnesses who testified to a person about something that he saw with his own eyes that it is not as he saw. He will never listen to them, but rather will know that they are false witnesses. Therefore the Torah said that (even if) the sign or the wonder comes true, do not listen to the words of that prophet. For, behold, he comes to you with a sign or a wonder to contradict what you saw with your own eyes. Since we do not believe in wonders unless the Torah tells us to, how can we accept this (false prophet's) sign to contradict the prophecy of Moshe Rabbeinu which we ourselves saw and heard?

In other words, any signs or wonders that our competitors may claim,[18] are worthless even if they actually happened,[19] because they cannot convince us to ignore that which we know positively to be the truth.

The Rambam continues further with his hidden agenda. Both Christianity and Islam agree that the Torah was once valid, but each one says that G-d changed his mind. Christianity claims that the Torah was abolished, and now all one needs to do is accept the belief in the Nazarene. Islam claims that Mohammed is Allah's new prophet, and all who do not accept him are condemned forever. Here, the Rambam tells us that this simply cannot be.

> רמב"ם הלכות יסודי התורה פרק ט הלכה א
>
> דבר ברור ומפורש בתורה שהיא מצוה עומדת לעולם ולעולמי עולמים אין לה לא שינוי ולא גרעון ולא תוספת שנאמר את כל הדבר אשר אנכי מצוה אתכם אותו תשמרון לעשות לא תוסף עליו ולא תגרע ממנו. ונאמר והנגלות לנו ולבנינו עד עולם לעשות את כל דברי התורה הזאת. הא למדת שכל דברי תורה מצווין אנו לעשותן עד עולם. וכן הוא אומר חוקת עולם לדורותיכם. ונאמר לא בשמים היא, הא למדת שאין נביא רשאי לחדש דבר מעתה. לפיכך

---

18 They generally make these claims without any historical substantiation whatsoever.

19 The Torah tells us clearly that a false prophet may be given the power to make a miracle in order to test our loyalty to Hashem. (*Devarim* 13:4).

Other Beliefs: Unproved and Unprovable

> אם יעמוד איש בין מן האומות בין מישראל ויעשה אות ומופת ויאמר שד'
> שלחו להוסיף מצוה או לגרוע מצוה או לפרש במצוה מן המצות פירוש שלא
> שמענו ממשה או שאמר שאותן המצות שנצטוו בהן ישראל אינן לעולם
> ולדורי דורות אלא מצות לפי זמן היו הרי זה נביא שקר שהרי בא להכחיש
> נבואתו של משה ומיתתו בחנק על שהזיד לדבר בשם ד' אשר לא צוהו שהוא
> ברוך שמו צוה למשה שהמצוה הזאת לנו ולבנינו עד עולם ולא איש ק-ל
> ויכזב.
>
> *It is clear and explicit in the Torah that it is a commandment which will stay forever and ever, not subject to change, subtraction or addition. As the pasuk says, "All the things I command you, guard to do. Do not add on to them and do not subtract from them." It (also) says, "The revealed things are for us and our children forever, to do all the words of this Torah." So you learn that we are commanded to keep all the words of this Torah forever. Therefore, if a man will arise, whether from the nations or from Yisrael, make a sign or a wonder and say that Hashem sent him to add or subtract a commandment, or (even) to explain a different explanation of a mitzvah than that which we heard from Moshe Rabbeinu, or if he tells us that those mitzvos which Yisrael was commanded to keep were not intended forever and for all generations, but only temporary, this person is a false prophet, for he comes to contradict the prophecy of Moshe Rabbeinu. His death shall be by strangulation for the audacity of speaking in the name of Hashem what He did not command him. For He, may His name be blessed, commanded to Moshe that this mitzvah (the Torah) is for us and for our children forever, and G-d is not a person, who tells lies.*

To sum up, there is no compelling reason to believe the claims of any religion whose origins were (supposedly) originally revealed in private. All the more so, when they contradict the faith that we received by Har Sinai before the eyes of three million witnesses, our ancestors. G-d doesn't change His mind, but if He did, He would have told us so publicly, before condemning us to hell for not believing in the new faith.

CHAPTER NINE

Yetzias Mitzrayim — the Eternal Testimony

The story of *yetzias Mitzrayim* is of the utmost importance in our *emunah*. It is emphasized throughout the *Chumash*, indeed throughout the entire Tanach. When we were given the Ten Commandments, the Creator introduced Himself as the G-d Who had taken us forth from Egypt.

> שמות פרק כ פסוק ב
> אָנֹכִי ד' אֱלֹקֶיךָ אֲשֶׁר הוֹצֵאתִיךָ מֵאֶרֶץ מִצְרַיִם מִבֵּית עֲבָדִים:
>
> I am Hashem, your G-d, who took you out from the land of Egypt.

Many mitzvos end with the words, "I am Hashem, your G-d, who took you out of the land of Mitzrayim." Concerning the mitzvah to have honest weights and scales, the Torah concludes with the following words:

> ויקרא יט פסוק לו
> מֹאזְנֵי צֶדֶק אַבְנֵי צֶדֶק אֵיפַת צֶדֶק וְהִין צֶדֶק יִהְיֶה לָכֶם אֲנִי ד' אֱלֹקֵיכֶם אֲשֶׁר הוֹצֵאתִי אֶתְכֶם מֵאֶרֶץ מִצְרָיִם:

> Honest scales, stone weights, dry and liquid measuring vessels you should have. I am Hashem, your G-d, who took you out from the land of Egypt.

Concerning the prohibition against taking interest on a loan, the Torah concludes in the same manner as before:

> ויקרא כה פסוק לה-לח
>
> וְכִי יָמוּךְ אָחִיךָ וּמָטָה יָדוֹ עִמָּךְ וְהֶחֱזַקְתָּ בּוֹ גֵּר וְתוֹשָׁב וָחַי עִמָּךְ: אַל תִּקַּח מֵאִתּוֹ נֶשֶׁךְ וְתַרְבִּית וְיָרֵאתָ מֵאֱלֹקֶיךָ וְחֵי אָחִיךָ עִמָּךְ: אֶת כַּסְפְּךָ לֹא תִתֵּן לוֹ בְּנֶשֶׁךְ וּבְמַרְבִּית לֹא תִתֵּן אָכְלֶךָ: אֲנִי ד' אֱלֹקֵיכֶם אֲשֶׁר הוֹצֵאתִי אֶתְכֶם מֵאֶרֶץ מִצְרַיִם לָתֵת לָכֶם אֶת אֶרֶץ כְּנַעַן לִהְיוֹת לָכֶם לֵאלֹקִים:

> When your brother will be poor and stretch out his hand to you (for help), you should hold him up. (Whether) a convert or a citizen he should have a living with you. Do not take from him interest or usury, and you shall fear from your G-d. Your brother shall have a living with you. Your money you shall not give with interest and your food you shall not give with usury. I am Hashem, your G-d, who took you out from the land of Egypt to give you the land of Canaan, to be to you for G-d.

One more example, concerning the mitzvah of *tzitzis*:

> במדבר טו פסוק לט-מא
>
> וְהָיָה לָכֶם לְצִיצִת וּרְאִיתֶם אֹתוֹ וּזְכַרְתֶּם אֶת כָּל מִצְוֹת ד' וַעֲשִׂיתֶם אֹתָם וְלֹא תָתוּרוּ אַחֲרֵי לְבַבְכֶם וְאַחֲרֵי עֵינֵיכֶם אֲשֶׁר אַתֶּם זֹנִים אַחֲרֵיהֶם: לְמַעַן תִּזְכְּרוּ וַעֲשִׂיתֶם אֶת כָּל מִצְוֹתָי וִהְיִיתֶם קְדֹשִׁים לֵאלֹקֵיכֶם: אֲנִי ד' אֱלֹקֵיכֶם אֲשֶׁר הוֹצֵאתִי אֶתְכֶם מֵאֶרֶץ מִצְרַיִם לִהְיוֹת לָכֶם לֵאלֹקִים אֲנִי ד' אֱלֹקֵיכֶם:

> They shall be to you for fringes. You will see them and remember all the commandments of Hashem and do them. You shall not stray after your heart and after your eyes, which you (tend to) stray after them. In order you shall remember and do all my mitzvos, and be holy to your G-d. I am Hashem, your G-d, who took you out of the land of Egypt to be to you for G-d. I am Hashem, your G-d.

One of the themes of Shabbos and *yamim tovim* is *zecher l'yetzias Mitzrayim* (a reminder of the Exodus from Egypt).

> **דברים פרק ה פסוק יב - טו**
>
> שָׁמוֹר אֶת־יוֹם הַשַּׁבָּת לְקַדְּשׁוֹ כַּאֲשֶׁר צִוְּךָ ד' אֱלֹקֶיךָ: שֵׁשֶׁת יָמִים תַּעֲבֹד וְעָשִׂיתָ כָּל־מְלַאכְתֶּךָ: וְיוֹם הַשְּׁבִיעִי שַׁבָּת לַיהֹוָה אֱלֹהֶיךָ לֹא־תַעֲשֶׂה כָל־מְלָאכָה אַתָּה וּבִנְךָ־וּבִתֶּךָ וְעַבְדְּךָ־וַאֲמָתֶךָ וְשׁוֹרְךָ וַחֲמֹרְךָ וְכָל־בְּהֶמְתֶּךָ וְגֵרְךָ אֲשֶׁר בִּשְׁעָרֶיךָ לְמַעַן יָנוּחַ עַבְדְּךָ וַאֲמָתְךָ כָּמוֹךָ: וְזָכַרְתָּ כִּי־עֶבֶד הָיִיתָ בְּאֶרֶץ מִצְרַיִם וַיֹּצִאֲךָ ד' אֱלֹקֶיךָ מִשָּׁם בְּיָד חֲזָקָה וּבִזְרֹעַ נְטוּיָה עַל־כֵּן צִוְּךָ ד' אֱלֹקֶיךָ לַעֲשׂוֹת אֶת־יוֹם הַשַּׁבָּת:
>
> *Guard the day of Shabbos to keep it holy, as Hashem, your G-d, has commanded you. Six days you shall serve and do all your work. The seventh day is a Shabbos to Hashem, your G-d. Do not do any work, you or your son and daughter, servant and maidservant, your ox, donkey, any of your animals, your converts who live in your gateways. In order that your servant and maidservant shall rest like you. You shall remember that you were a slave in the land of Egypt and Hashem took you out from there with a strong hand and an outstretched arm. Therefore Hashem has commanded you to make the day of Shabbos.*

Undoubtedly, one reason for this emphasis is that we were redeemed from slavery to become the servants of Hashem. We owe Him our obedience because He redeemed us from bondage. However, there is another very important reason, one which has much to do with our subject. Let's let the Ramban tell it to us in his own words.

> **רמב״ן שמות פרק י״ג פסוק ט״ז (באמצע דבור המתחיל ולטוטפות)**
>
> ועתה אומר לך כלל בטעם מצות רבות. הנה מעת היות ע״ג בעולם מימי אנוש החלו הדעות להשתבש באמונה. מהם כופרים בעיקר ואומרים כי העולם קדמון כחשו בד' ויאמרו לא הוא. ומהם מכחישים בידיעתו הפרטית ואמרו איכה ידע ק-ל ויש דעה בעליון (תהלים עג יא). ומהם שיודו בידיעה ומכחישים בהשגחה ויעשו אדם כדגי הים שלא ישגיח הק-ל בהם ואין עמהם עונש או שכר יאמרו עזב ד' את הארץ. וכאשר ירצה האלקים בעדה או ביחיד ויעשה עמהם מופת בשנוי מנהגו של עולם וטבעו יתברר לכל בטול הדעות האלה כלם. כי המופת הנפלא מורה שיש לעולם אלו-ה מחדשו ויודע ומשגיח ויכול. וכאשר יהיה המופת ההוא נגזר תחלה מפי נביא יתברר ממנו עוד אמתת הנבואה כי ידבר האלקים את האדם ויגלה סודו אל עבדיו הנביאים ותתקיים עם זה התורה כלה:
>
> *Now I will tell you a principle concerning the reasons behind many mitzvos. Behold! From the time that there was avodah zarah in the world, from the days of Enosh, ideas about emunah began to be distorted. Some of*

the people denied the fundamental principle of the existence of a Creator. They said that the world had always existed, denied Hashem, and said He does not exist. Others denied His knowledge of the detailed happenings of this world. They said, "How can G-d know, and there be knowledge to the One above?" Others admitted that G-d knows, but they denied Divine Providence. They consider mankind like the fish of the sea, that G-d does not supervise them and there is no punishment or reward for them. They say that G-d has deserted the world.

When Hashem favors a community or an individual and does with them a wonder by changing the natural running of the world, it becomes clear to all that these ideas are all false. The marvelous wonder shows that the world has a G-d who created it new, Who knows, supervises and is capable of doing anything. Should that wonder be announced in advance by a prophet, then also the truth of prophecy has been made clear, that G-d speaks to people and reveals His secrets to His servants the prophets. Thereby the entire Torah is substantiated.

Ramban continues:

ולכן יאמר הכתוב במופתים למען תדע כי אני ד' בקרב הארץ (שמות פרק ח' פסוק י"ח) להורות על ההשגחה כי לא עזב אותה למקרים כדעתם. ואמר (שם ט כט) למען תדע כי לד' הארץ להורות על החידוש כי הם שלו שבראם מאין ואמר (שם פרק ט' פסוק י"ד) בעבור תדע כי אין כמוני בכל הארץ להורות על היכולת שהוא שליט בכל אין מעכב בידו כי בכל זה היו המצריים מכחישים או מסתפקים. אם כן האותות והמופתים הגדולים עדים נאמנים באמונת הבורא ובתורה כלה:

Therefore the verse says about the miracles, "In order that you shall know that I am Hashem right here on the earth," to demonstrate the Divine Providence, that Hashem did not desert the world to haphazard occurrences, as they thought. It says, "In order that you shall know that the earth belongs to Hashem," to demonstrate that He made the world from new and all is His, for He created them as something from nothing. It says, "In order that you should know that there is none like Me in all the earth," to demonstrate (His) ability, that He is in control of everything, and no one can restrain Him. All of this the Egyptians denied or were in doubt about.

Ramban continues:

> ובעבור כי הקב"ה לא יעשה אות ומופת בכל דור לעיני כל רשע או כופר, יצוה אותנו שנעשה תמיד זכרון ואות לאשר ראו עינינו ונעתיק הדבר אל בנינו ובניהם לבניהם ובניהם לדור אחרון.
>
> Since Hakadosh Baruch Hu will not make a sign or a wonder in every generation to the eyes of every rasha or scoffer, He commanded us that we should make constant reminders and signs to that which our eyes saw, and transmit this thing to our children and their children, to their children and grandchildren until the very last generation.

Ramban continues:

> והחמיר מאד בענין הזה כמו שחייב כרת באכילת חמץ (לעיל יב טו) ובעזיבת הפסח (במדבר ט יג). והצריך שנכתוב כל מה שנראה אלינו באותות ובמופתים על ידינו ועל בין עינינו ולכתוב אותו עוד על פתחי הבתים במזוזות ושנזכיר זה בפינו בבקר ובערב וכו' ושנעשה סוכה בכל שנה וכן כל כיוצא בהן מצות רבות זכר ליציאת מצרים. והכל להיות לנו בכל הדורות עדות במופתים שלא ישתכחו, ולא יהיה פתחון פה לכופר להכחיש אמונת האלקים.
>
> The Torah was very strict concerning this, even giving a penalty of kareis for eating chametz and for neglecting to bring the korban Pesach. It requires us to write all the signs and wonders that we saw on our arms and between our eyes, and also to write it on the doorways of our homes in mezuzos, and to mention it with our mouths in the morning and in the evening... to make a sukkah every year, and all such similar things. All of this is so that we will testify about the miracles throughout the generations, so that they shall not be forgotten. The scoffer will not be able to open his mouth to deny the belief in G-d.

> כי הקונה מזוזה בזוז אחד וקבעה בפתחו ונתכוון בענינה כבר הודה בחדוש העולם ובידיעת הבורא והשגחתו וגם בנבואה והאמין בכל פנות התורה:
>
> Because the person who buys a mezuzah for a zuz and affixes it in his doorway, and thinks about its meaning, has already admitted to the creation of the world, the Creator's knowledge and intervention, in prophecy and in all the fundamentals of our Torah.

Ramban tells us clearly how the *makkos* demonstrated not only that the Creator exists, but also that He knows all and controls everything on earth. The water, the frogs, the bugs, the animals and all the forces of Nature are all totally in His hands. On this, too, we have an unbroken *mesorah* since the very first generation. The first Seder was held in Jewish homes the night before the Exodus from Egypt. They discussed the miracles and plagues that had occurred before their very eyes. The next year they added in the Crossing of the Red Sea and *matan Torah*. We have never stopped making the Seder ever since that night. Wherever Jews have lived, they made the Seder and commemorated all the things that the first generation testified that they had seen with their own eyes.

CHAPTER TEN

Who Wrote All This?

The ideas presented above are the pillar upon which the faith of *Klal Yisrael* stands. They are incontrovertible, with no room to budge to the left or the right. However, the more *chizuk* the better. Hence we will move on to a very different method of showing that indeed the Torah is the word of Hashem Yisborach Himself.

The *mishnah* in *Pirkei Avos* tells us that we should know what to answer to the *apikorus*. Reb Avigdor Miller said that he heard from his *rebbi* in the Slobodka Yeshiva that this refers also to the little *apikorus* inside each one of us. Every person may at some time of weakness in his life experience doubts and need some fortification to his *emunah*. We hope to offer some of that fortification now.

ZOOLOGY, ASTRONOMY, GEOGRAPHY

Our Torah is not merely a law book with a historical narrative. Because it is the *d'var Hashem*, it is infinite. The deeper you delve, the more information you find. Many astounding things contained in our Torah could not conceivably have been written by a human hand. How could the Torah make broad, sweeping statements about things that require knowledge of the entire globe, the heavens and the future? Only the Creator himself could have made such statements! Here we will present a few of them. Then we will ask ourselves, who could have written all this? First, however, let us view a very fundamental statement from Ramban.

A TORAH WHICH CONTAINS ALL BRANCHES OF KNOWLEDGE

Ramban, in a lengthy introduction to his commentary on *Chumash*, tells us that when Hashem gave the Torah to Moshe Rabbeinu, He revealed to him all the wisdom of the universe: knowledge of plants and trees, fish and birds, the stars and planets, ad infinitum. We quote here just a short excerpt from this enlightening introduction.

> רמב"ן הקדמה לספר בראשית
>
> הודיעו תחלה ענין בריאת שמים וארץ וכל צבאם ... וכח צמחי האדמה ונפש התנועה ונפש המדבר... לגלגלים ולשמים וצבאיהם... ושלמה המלך עליו השלום שנתן לו האלקים החכמה והמדע הכל מן התורה היה לו וממנה למד עד שידע סוד כל התולדות ... עד שכתב אפילו ספר רפואות

Hashem first informed him (Moshe Rabbeinu) all about the creation of heaven and earth and all that is contained in them... the power of the plants of the ground, the moving creatures (animals) and the speaking beings (humans)... the galaxies, the heavens and all that is contained in them... and Shlomo haMelech, of blessed memory, to whom Hashem gave wisdom and knowledge, all of it came to him from the Torah. From it he learned until he knew the secret qualities of all existing things... until he even wrote a book of cures (for all sicknesses).

KOSHER AND NON-KOSHER ANIMALS

The Torah commands us to eat only of the animals which have two signs of *kashrus*: those with split hooves and who chew their cud. All other animals are forbidden to eat. It would seem that if nothing more than that were said, we would have all the necessary instructions. Nevertheless, the Torah goes out of its way to enumerate the four species which have only one of the two signs of *kashrus*:

> **ויקרא יא פסוק ד-ח**
>
> אך את זה לא תאכלו ממעלי הגרה וממפרסי הפרסה את הגמל כי מעלה גרה הוא ופרסה איננו מפריס טמא הוא לכם: ואת השפן כי מעלה גרה הוא ופרסה לא יפריס טמא הוא לכם: ואת הארנבת כי מעלת גרה הוא ופרסה לא הפריסה טמאה הוא לכם: ואת החזיר כי מפריס פרסה הוא ושסע שסע פרסה והוא גרה לא יגר טמא הוא לכם: מבשרם לא תאכלו ובנבלתם לא תגעו טמאים הם לכם:
>
> But these you may not eat, from the ones that bring up their cud or that have split hooves: The camel, for it brings up its cud but does not have split hooves; and the hare, for it brings up its cud but does not have split hooves; and the rabbit for it brings up its cud but does not have split hooves; and the pig, for it does have split hooves but does not chew its cud. From their flesh you may not eat and do not approach their carcass. They are defiled for you. (Vayikra 11:4–8)

Ramban makes it clear that the intention of these verses is to tell you that these are the only four which have only one of the two signs of *kashrus*.

> **רמב"ן ויקרא יא פסוק ג**
>
> כל מפרסת פרסה ושוסעת שסע פרסות מעלת גרה. טעם הכתוב הזה שכל בהמה שיהיו בה שני הסימנין הללו תאכל, אבל לא תאכלו באחד מהם. והיה ראוי שיאמר כן בדרך כלל, אלא שפרט הגמל והשפן והארנבת בגרה והחזיר בפרסה, מפני שאין אחרים בעולם בסימן האחד לבדו:
>
> "All that have split hooves and bring up the cud": The meaning of the verse is that all that have these two signs you may eat, but with only one (sign) you may not eat. It would have been fitting for the Torah to tell us this in a general way (without specifying the names of the four species), but the Torah singled out the camel, hare, and rabbit that bring up the cud, and the pig that has (split) hooves because there are no others in the world that have only one sign (of kashrus). (Ramban, Vayikra 11:3)

From here the Sages see an amazing proof that the Torah is from Hashem:

> **חולין דף נט עמוד א**
>
> דתנא דבי רבי ישמעאל ואת החזיר כי מפריס פרסה הוא שליט בעולמו יודע שאין לך דבר שמפריס פרסה וטמא אלא חזיר לפיכך פרט בו הכתוב:

> The Tana in the yeshiva of Rabbi Yishmael taught, "The ruler of His world knows that there is nothing else that has split hooves and is still non-kosher (because it does not chew its cud), therefore it specified it." (Chulin 59a)

This is really quite astonishing. The Torah was written at a time when most of the continents on the globe were as yet unknown to the civilized world. Australia was only discovered a mere three hundred years ago, and America only five hundred years ago. Thousands of wildlife species have been discovered that were totally unknown to the ancient civilized world. Why would any writer (other than Hashem Yisborach) want to put himself out on a limb by making such a rash, unnecessary, and unfounded proclamation? How could the Torah know that never, ever would there be found a fifth species that has only one sign of *kashrus*?[20] Here we are, a few thousand years later, and the prediction still holds true. "From here there is an answer to those that say the Torah is not from Heaven."

PLENTY OF FISH IN THE SEA

The Torah sets two criteria for a fish to be kosher: It must have: (1) overlapping scales, and (2) fins. Any fish that do not have both of these features are forbidden to be eaten.

Imagine that you are fishing on one end of a long pier. A fisherman far down the other end lands a rather large fish, cuts off some pieces, and leaves the pier. You decide to go and investigate. Curiously enough, the fish he caught is a species you have never seen before. It does have overlapping scales, but you don't know if it had fins, because the sections of the body where the fins might have been were cut away. The Mishnah teaches that you may eat this fish, because it definitely had fins — because all fish that have scales have fins. That means there isn't a single fish in any of the oceans, seas or rivers in the entire world that has scales and no fins. Eat and enjoy! The fish is kosher!

---

20 There is some discrepancy raised by modern writers as to the exact identification of the *shafan* and the *arneves*. However, this has been cleared up in a recently published book by Dr. Yizchak Betech, Dr. Obadia Maya, and TOV's international staff, *The Enigma of the Biblical Shafan*, 2013, published by TOV.

> מסכת נדה נ"א ע"ב
>
> כל שיש לו קשקשת יש לו סנפיר ויש שיש לו סנפיר ואין לו קשקשת.
>
> Any (fish) that has scales has fins. There are those that have fins but no scales. (Niddah 51b)

This statement was made when the civilized world did not know of the existence of the Pacific Ocean and countless other bodies of water. Certainly, no one had ever explored the depths of even the oceans and seas they were familiar with. Since that time, with the advent of modern equipment, tens of thousands of previously unknown marine species have been discovered. Amazingly enough, not a single one has scales but no fins. Who wrote that statement? Who could have written it?

Note that the proof here is twofold. First of all, how could any human being, then, know about the future discovery — or lack thereof — of animals and fish thousands of years later? Second, why would any human author write in his book things that were likely to prove the book false? Artificial religions do everything they can to avoid being caught, and here, again and again, the Torah is going out of its way to make incredible claims that can only have been true if they were made by G-d Himself!

TWINKLE, TWINKLE ZILLION STARS

Less than ten thousand stars are visible to the naked eye. Up until the invention of the telescope by Galileo about four hundred years ago, no other stars were known. After Galileo, it was known that there are many more, but it was assumed that there was no galaxy other than the Milky Way. By now, clusters of galaxies and clusters of those clusters ("superclusters" with large voids in between them) have been discovered. The 2005 Encyclopedia Britannica[21] states: "Of the trillions of stars comprising the universe, many occur in pairs, multiple systems and clusters." Long before Galileo and the invention of the telescope, the Sages of the Talmud knew that there are an astounding number of stars and that they are situated in clusters and superclusters. Consider, then, this Gemara:

---

21 "Stars and Star Clusters."

> **מסכת ברכות לב**
>
> (ישעיהו מ"ט) ותאמר ציון עזבני ד' וד' שכחני. ... אמר לה הקדוש ברוך הוא: בתי שנים עשר מזלות בראתי ברקיע ועל כל מזל ומזל בראתי לו שלשים חיל ועל כל חיל וחיל בראתי לו שלשים לגיון ועל כל לגיון ולגיון בראתי לו שלשים רהטון ועל כל רהטון ורהטון בראתי לו שלשים קרטון ועל כל קרטון וקרטון בראתי לו שלשים גסטרא ועל כל גסטרא וגסטרא תליתי בו שלש מאות וששים וחמשה אלפי רבוא כוכבים כנגד ימות החמה וכולן לא בראתי אלא בשבילך ואת אמרת עזבתני ושכחתני?
>
> *The pasuk (Isaiah 49) says, "Tzion said, 'Hashem has deserted me and Hashem has forgotten me" ... (Hashem) said to her, "My daughter, I created twelve constellations in the heavens. For each constellation I created thirty armies. To each army I created thirty legions. To each legion I created thirty brigades. To each brigade I created thirty battalions. In each battalion I hung three hundred sixty-five thousand myriads (ten thousands, equaling three billion six hundred fifty million) stars to correspond to the days in the solar year. All of them I created only for your sake, and you say, 'You have deserted and forgotten me.'"*

The total number of stars in the Gemara's calculation is about 10^{18}. Perhaps it will make a deeper impression if we put it into numbers: 10,000,000,000,000,000,000. That's ten million trillion. An astronomer living at any time after the writing of the Talmud, until about four hundred years ago, would have laughed upon hearing such a statement. Today, this figure is right in line with the most recent estimates. How did *Chazal* know this? Did the Sages have hidden conservatories with modern day telescopes? Was it a lucky guess? Or perhaps, this information was given as part of the Torah package from the *Borei Olam*?[22]

THE WORLD IS ROUND

Up until about five hundred years ago, people assumed the world was flat, and that one could actually fall off the edge (wherever it may be). Some

---

[22] From *Universe Today*, May 2014: "According to astronomers, there are probably more than 170 billion galaxies in the observable Universe, stretching out into a region of space 13.8 billion light-years away from us in all directions. And so, if you multiply the number of stars in our galaxy by the number of galaxies in the Universe, you get approximately 10^{24} stars. That's a one followed by twenty-four zeros. That's a septillion stars. But there could be more than that."

people believed that the world was supported on the backs of three gigantic elephants. With Columbus' discovery of America, people began to believe that the world is round like a ball. Today, of course, we have all seen pictures, and indeed the world is round. However, the *chachmei Yisrael* always knew from their *mesorah* that this is the case. The Zohar was dictated about two thousand years ago, and these facts were known then.

> זוהר חדש בראשית טו
>
> אמר רבי יוסי ... כבר תנינא ממאריהון דמתיבתא דעלמא סגלגל הוא כדורא דא
>
> Rabbi Yosi said ... "We have already learned from the heads of the Yeshiva that the world is round like a ball."

The Midrash, as well, when explaining the gifts which the *nesi'im* brought to dedicate the Mishkan, makes the following statement:

> מדרש רבה במדבר נשא יג
>
> מזרק אחד כסף. כנגד העולם שהוא עשוי כדור הנזרק מיד ליד
>
> (The cup for sprinkling the blood was) one mizrak of silver, which represents the world which is round like a ball, which is thrown from hand to hand (zarak means thrown).

Did the Sages have satellites to take pictures of the world and discover that it is round? Or did they know it as part of the information they were handed down from Har Sinai?

EARTH REVOLVES ON ITS AXIS

About five hundred years ago, the scientist Copernicus discovered that the earth revolves on its axis, and that is what causes the switch from day to night. The side facing the sun has day, the opposite side has night. But fifteen hundred years earlier, the *Zohar Hakadosh* already recorded this information.

> זוהר הקדוש ויקרא י
>
> ובספרא דרב המנונא סבא פריש יתיר דהא כל ישובא מתגלגלא בעגולא כדור אלין לתתא ואלין לעילא וכל אינון בריין משניין בחזוויהו משנויא דאויר כפום כל אתר ואתר וקיימין בקיומייהו כשאר בני נשא

> *In the sefer of Rav Hamnuna Saba, he explains even more, that the entire world revolves in a circle, with these on bottom and these on top, and all these creatures differ in their appearance because of the different atmosphere, according to each and every place, but they remain in their existence like all other people.*

> ועל דא אית אתר בישובא כד נהיר לאלין חשיך לאלין לאלין יממא ולאלין ליליא
>
> *And therefore there are places in civilization when it is light for these it is dark for these. For these it is day and for these it is night.*

> ואית אתר דכוליה יממא ולא אשתכח ביה ליליא בר משעתא חדא זעירא
>
> *And there is a place which is completely daytime and there is no nighttime found there except for one short hour.*

From the above excerpts from the Zohar and the Midrash, we see that the Sages had knowledge of numerous things that were unknown to the world at large two thousand years ago:

1. The world is round.
2. The world revolves on its axis.
3. For this reason, when it is light on one side of the world it is dark on the other side.
4. There is a bottom and a top to the world. (The Southern Hemisphere was completely unknown to the ancients living in the Northern Hemisphere. Australia was discovered a mere three hundred years ago).
5. People living on the bottom do not fall off, but rather "remain in their existence like all other people (gravity)."
6. The differences in people's appearance are the result of the varying atmospheres.
7. There are places that are almost always light. (This is obviously referring to the North and South Poles.)

Ask your local skeptic how this could have been known without it being revealed through prophecy. *Ma'aminim b'nei ma'aminim* know from the *mesorah* that our Torah comes from the *Borei Olam*, but as we've already said, additional *chizuk* is always of benefit.

CHAPTER ELEVEN

He Knows in Advance

Quite astonishing, this Torah of ours. In the Tanach, Hashem is referred to as "He who tells the end from the very beginning," and also by the title, "the One Who proclaims the generation from the start." In addition to revealing secrets about the natural world, the Torah is full of predictions for the future. All of these predictions have come through to the letter, except for those that refer to the end of the *galus* and the coming of Mashiach. Those are yet to come. Let's take a look at a few of them, let the amazement sink in, and realize that we are hearing the words of the Creator.

> ישעיה מא פסוק ד
>
> מִי פָעַל וְעָשָׂה קֹרֵא הַדֹּרוֹת מֵרֹאשׁ אֲנִי ד' רִאשׁוֹן וְאֶת אַחֲרֹנִים אֲנִי הוּא׃
>
> Who has wrought and done (all this)? (It is) the One Who calls the generations in advance. I, Hashem, am first, and I am with the last.

> ישעיה מו פסוק ט-י
>
> זִכְרוּ רִאשֹׁנוֹת מֵעוֹלָם כִּי אָנֹכִי קֵ-ל וְאֵין עוֹד אֱלֹקִים וְאֶפֶס כָּמוֹנִי׃
> מַגִּיד מֵרֵאשִׁית אַחֲרִית וּמִקֶּדֶם אֲשֶׁר לֹא נַעֲשׂוּ אֹמֵר עֲצָתִי תָקוּם וְכָל חֶפְצִי אֶעֱשֶׂה׃

> *I tell the end from the very beginning, and before the things are done I say that My plan will stand, and all I desire I will do.*

In these verses, the *Navi* tells us that Hashem makes it all happen according to His desire. He is in full control of everything that transpires, but merely told us in advance what He would choose to do later on.

THE TOCHACHAH: IF YOU STRAY, THEN...

When *Am Yisrael* entered into a covenant with Hashem, they made a deal. If they will keep the Torah, they will be on top of the world. They will be the most powerful and affluent nation on earth, a *mamleches kohanim v'goy kadosh* (a nation of nobles and a holy nation). All other nations will revere them and will know that only the Jewish people had the truth all along. No nation will even contemplate starting up with them. These blessings are all outlined in two places: one section in *parshas Bechukosai* and a second in *parshas Ki Savo*. Because we were mostly worthy of these blessings in the days of Dovid haMelech and Shlomo haMelech, they were fulfilled almost completely. In the era of Mashiach, we will be worthy of the blessings in their entirety.

There is another side of the coin, however. That is the section following the *berachos*, wherein the Torah forewarns us of the consequences of breaking the contract that we "signed" at Har Sinai. Interestingly, our forefathers entered into a special *bris* two separate times: once when they were still encamped by Har Sinai, and once at the end of the forty year stay in the desert, by the plains of Moav. Each time they were told what would befall them if they deviate from Hashem's path, and they swore to keep it. There is, however, a seemingly very difficult problem here. In *Bechukosai*, the Torah predicts one set of consequences, and in *Ki Savo* the predictions are very different. Isn't this a contradiction?

RAMBAN SHEDS LIGHT ON THE MYSTERY

Ramban, in his commentary on *Chumash*, answers the question in a most astounding way. From the insights provided by Ramban, we will see how the Torah predicted the future of *Am Yisrael* down to the last detail.

Only the Creator, in whose hands is the destiny of all creatures, could have predicted all this in advance.

Ramban answers: The two predictions are not identical because they refer to two different future episodes. The *tochachah* in *Bechukosai* is an accurate, step-by-step prediction of *churban Bayis Rishon* (the destruction of the first Beis Hamikdash), whereas the *tochachah* in *Ki Savo* is an exact description of what will occur at the time of *churban Bayis Sheini* (the destruction of the second Beis Hamikdash). Now, when we review the history of these two tragic events, and realize that the Torah foresaw everything way in advance, we will have a great source of *chizuk* that Torah is indeed *min haShamayim*.

Before we go through the Ramban, however, and see that all the details of both destructions were all predicted, let's take a look at something much closer to our time: the foretelling of the events of the *galus* that we are in today.

TWO THOUSAND YEARS OF GALUS

The Torah not only told us what would happen at the time of the *churban* (as we will soon see), but also what would subsequently occur in the long and bitter *galus* that we've had to endure. Many of the things we've gone through are a total mystery to us. They don't seem to make any sense, and we simply don't know why it should logically be so. Nevertheless, the Torah foretold it all, and it has all come true "to the letter." Incredibly, in four short verses, the Torah foretold the destiny of two thousand years.

A LITTLE HISTORY

After the destruction of the *Bayis Sheini*, Jews became dispersed throughout the Roman Empire, eventually reaching all corners of the earth. They never became very numerous. Persecution, pogroms and other circumstances saw to that. Almost invariably, the Jew became the scapegoat of his host society. Special discriminative laws severely limited the avenues through which Jews could earn a living. Jews were never totally secure in their host countries. Even after long periods of quiet and relative tranquility, the wheel of fortune would turn on them.

Then they would be persecuted, vilified, and very often chased out of their homes with nowhere to go. Jews were hardly ever able to put up a serious defense against their enemies. They were basically outnumbered and without weapons, which made fighting back a futile effort. This is, in short, the general pattern of our *galus* experience for just under the last two thousand years. Now let's see how this was all foretold in advance, detail by detail.

SMALL IN NUMBER

It is hard to estimate exactly how many millions of Jews were in the world at the time of the *churban*.[23] The Chinese people also had numerous millions at that time. For some reason, although today the Chinese number close to one-and-a-half billion, the Jewish people never got too populous. The Jews still number only about fourteen million. Other peoples grow over the centuries, but not we. Whenever the Jewish people reach a certain minimal peak, something always happens to maintain or diminish their numbers. The Torah told us in advance that this would be the case.

> דברים כח פסוק סב
> ונשארתם במתי מעט תחת אשר הייתם ככוכבי השמים לרב כי לא שמעת בקול ד' אלקיך:
>
> You will remain small in population, instead of what you were, like the stars of the heavens for many. Because you didn't listen to the voice of Hashem, your G-d.

ANTI-SEMITISM

Anti-Semitism is really a great mystery. Many books have been written to explain why the nations of the world have directed so much hatred toward us. After all, we are a pretty good people. Jews have made extraordinary contributions to the world in commerce, medicine, science, astronomy and technology. Any country where Jews lived has benefited greatly from

---

23 From descriptions in the Talmud, it is obvious that they must have been a few million.

their presence. With very few exceptions, we are a non-violent people, with very little drunkenness, theft and immorality. Most Jews are law-abiding citizens. We don't even differ so greatly from other peoples in our external appearance. Yet the persistent hatred we have endured is unequaled by any other people. Why?

Many rationales have been offered to explain anti-Semitism. The excuse changes according to the circumstances. When we are rich and prosperous, others are jealous of us. When we are poor, others look down on us. When the nations were very devoted to their religions, they hated us because we refused to accept their beliefs; we (supposedly) killed their god or rejected their (so-called) prophet. When nations began turning to secularism, Jews began to feel that anti-Semitism was coming to an end. No such thing! Totally unexpected, a new brand of anti-Semitism arose, not based on religion, but merely on race. They hate us just because we are not of their race. It makes no sense at all. So if we can't make sense out of it in retrospect, surely no one could have predicted it in advance. But here it is, right in the *pasuk*.

> דברים כח פסוק סג
> והיה כאשר שש ד' עליכם להיטיב אתכם ולהרבות אתכם כן ישיש ד' עליכם להאביד אתכם ולהשמיד אתכם
>
> *And it will be, that just as Hashem rejoiced over you to do good to you and to increase you, so shall He cause others to rejoice over you to destroy you and to wipe you out.*

The Ribono shel Olam tells us not to try to figure it out. There will be no satisfactory explanation for it. They will hate you because it is so decreed by Hashem. The circumstances will not make any difference. He will cause them to hate you. It is part of the *galus* package.

SCATTERED AROUND THE GLOBE

When a nation is conquered by another nation, many different things can result. The conquering nation may annihilate the conquered or may banish them to some other land. (Sancheriv, king of Ashur, did so to the ten tribes of

Yisrael, and to all the other nations he conquered.) Perhaps, as often happens, the two nations intermingle and eventually become one. Why would the Torah predict that *Klal Yisrael* will be scattered from one end of the earth to the other? Why should this happen? Indeed, that is precisely what happened. Jews have lived almost everywhere on the globe. Today one can find Jewish communities in Australia, Africa, North and South America, Europe and Asia. Hurry up and you can still catch *Minchah* in Melbourne, Johannesburg, Tokyo, St. Louis, Buenos Aires or Zurich. There are many more places that had large Jewish communities up until just recently. Jews have been everywhere. There was no reason at all for anyone to predict this, except for the Creator, who calls all the shots of history and has the power to make them all come true.[24]

> דברים כח פסוק סד
>
> והפיצך ד' בכל העמים מקצה הארץ ועד קצה הארץ:
>
> And Hashem will scatter you from one end of the earth to the other end of the earth.

WOOD AND STONE

In the second half of this last *pasuk*, we are told that we will indeed succumb to the temptations of the other religions.

> המשך פסוק סד
>
> ועבדת שם אלהים אחרים אשר לא ידעת אתה ואבתיך עץ ואבן:
>
> And you will worship there other gods that you and your forefathers never knew (before), wood and stone.

---

[24] There are other nations that are also widely dispersed around the globe, such as the Chinese people. However, their experience is quite different from ours in a number of ways. Their dispersion was never predicted, as was ours in the verses quoted here. Had their dispersion been predicted three thousand years ago, it also would have been astounding. The scattering of the Chinese involves only a relatively small percentage of Chinese people who no longer live in their ancestral homeland. In contrast, we were told that we would be sent into an exile that would end in a global-wide dispersion, with almost no Jews left in our land. Unlike other nations who have been recently dispersed, we have been scattered around the world for well over two thousand years, but still maintain the identity of a separate community. It is one of the conditions of our exile, exactly as told to us in our *Torah*.

Untold numbers of Jews have been lost to their heritage due to the work of missionaries or the pressure of governments. Interestingly enough, the symbol of Christianity is the wooden cross, while the symbol of Islam is the stone at Mecca. Yet the Torah insists that the Jewish nation will not disappear. There will still be a Jewish people around to be redeemed at the end of the *galus*. Two thousand years of pressure to assimilate cannot alter that.

PERSECUTION AND BANISHMENT

The following *pasuk* contains two distinct predictions. Wherever Jews are dispersed, they will have a rough time. They will not be at ease. They will be discriminated against, scorned and attacked. Sadly enough, this is exactly what happened. The Jews were taxed more heavily and more often than their gentile neighbors, in spite of the fact that Jews were almost always restricted from most sources of livelihood. Each place that we lived in had its own set of restrictive laws and practices that made our lives difficult and sometimes unbearable. In Western Europe, Jews were forced to live in narrow ghettos. The ghetto was seldom allowed to be enlarged, even when the Jewish population increased. The Jewish community could not build out, so they built upward, adding more and more stories to the existing buildings. The narrow streets became darker and darker because the sunlight was blocked out. Often, the government restricted the right to marry, so that the Jewish population would not explode. Sometimes only one child per family was granted a marriage license. Many cities charged a special Jewish head-tax for any Jew that wanted to gain entrance to the city. Often, staying overnight was forbidden to a Jew in many cities. If a Christian attacked a Jew, the law did nothing. If the Jew fought back, he was accused of attacking a "good Christian." Self-defense was almost never an excuse. The church regularly incited the mobs to hate Jews, boycott their businesses and attack the ghettos. In Eastern Europe there were no ghettos, but there was no lack of restrictions. Jews were forced to live only in a strip of Russia along its Western border. This strip was called the Pale of Settlement. Almost no Jews were allowed to live in the vast interior of Russia. Most types of livelihoods were off-limits for Jews. They were allowed to manufacture whiskey and vodka, but then, of course, the Russians blamed them for the widespread alcoholism in Russia. They were allowed to be moneylenders, but were blamed for the interest they needed to charge in order to make a living. The list goes on and on. We can't make much sense out of it, but here it is, spelled out for us in this next *pasuk*.

> דברים כ"ח פסוק ס"ה
> ובגוים ההם לא תרגיע ולא יהיה מנוח לכף רגלך:
>
> *And among those nations you shall not be at ease, nor will there be a resting place for the sole of your foot.*

This is the message of the second part of the *pasuk*: No foreign home will have permanence for you. "There will not be a resting place for the sole of your foot," but rather, you'll have to keep moving on. Tragically, the second half of this *pasuk* has also been fulfilled to the letter. (Jews were often nicknamed "the wandering Jew.") Jews were banished (or forced by circumstances) to migrate from almost every country in Europe at some time. No Jew was allowed in England, on pain of death, for three hundred years. The great French Jewish community was expelled from France. Communities in Germany were constantly seeking the Emperor's permission to banish their Jews, and usually received it. No home was to prove permanent. Great Sephardic communities lived in the Arab countries up until recently. Syria, Iraq, Iran and Morocco no longer have thriving Jewish settlements. They were persecuted when the State of Israel was declared, and had to flee while leaving all their possessions behind. Jews had originally been invited to Poland, and had lived there for a thousand years, up until the Holocaust, but the Poles picketed them with signs saying, "Jews, go home!" This has been the pattern for two thousand years.[25] Who could have known this in advance, if not the Creator?

---

25 There were exceptions to the pattern of discrimination. There was a "golden era" in Spain where Jews lived in relative comfort and security. Likewise, in the United States, Jews have experienced unprecedented equality, especially in the last fifty years or so. Nevertheless, the discriminations and persecutions are the general pattern of our history throughout the long and bitter exile.

> ולא יהיה מנוח לכף רגלך.
>
> *There will not be a resting placed for the sole of your foot.*

WHERE WAS THE OLD BRAVERY?

Throughout the long and bitter exile, the Jew has generally been known to be a meek, frightened "scaredy-cat." They "went like sheep to the slaughter" and put up relatively little resistance. True, they were unarmed and vastly outnumbered. We dare not think disparagingly of them because of this. Still, one would have expected them to put up a better fight. It wasn't always this way. Jews were known for tremendous bravery during the turmoil of the second Beis Hamikdash era. They gave the Romans a very hard time during a long war that lasted several years, with the Romans finally destroying the Beis Hamikdash. In the Bar Kochba revolution against Rome (sixty-two years after the *churban*) it was the same. A national personality trait should not undergo such a drastic change because of exile.

The question extends yet further. Since large numbers of Jews have returned to Eretz Yisrael, we once again see the bravery and *chutzpah* of old. They're not afraid of anyone and have performed many daring feats since the inception of the state. It doesn't really seem to make sense. A meek nature is something built in to the national character. It should be apparent wherever they are. Yet, this is exactly what the *pasuk* foretells here.

> ונתן ד' לך שם לב רגז וכליון עינים ודאבון נפש:
>
> *And Hashem will give you there a trembling heart, despair and anguish.*

There, in *galus*, Hashem will give you a trembling heart. You didn't have it before, and you won't have it when you return.

WHY WOULD ANYONE PREDICT THIS? HOW COULD ANYONE KNOW IT WOULD BE SO?

In these verses, the Torah foresaw in detail the conditions of our two thousand year exile. None of these things were predictable in advance.

Not by "educated guesses" or even by "lucky guesses." There was simply no reason to predict that the Jewish people would remain constantly small in number and not multiply like other nations. The Jewish people contributed so much to their host societies and should have earned the gratitude and respect of their gentile neighbors. No matter how good things were for a while (such as during the Golden Era in Spain), the wheel of fortune turned on them, and they were once again persecuted. After a people has been living somewhere for hundreds of years (even a thousand) it would seem likely to assume that they would remain there permanently, not be exiled time after time. According to our tradition, the Torah was given over three thousand years ago. This was hundreds — and thousands — of years before any of this 'history' actually happened.[26] Yet it was all predicted.

CONTRADICTORY PREDICTIONS

Not only can we not fathom why or how anyone (except Hashem Yisborach) could make such predictions, but some of the predictions even seem to contradict one another. If, as predicted, the Jews will remain small in number, be persecuted, and also succumb to the temptations of the hosts' religions, then it would make sense to also predict that after a while there will be no more Jewish people. No such thing, the Torah says. All this will happen, nevertheless there will still be a Jewish people to be redeemed with the coming of Mashiach, as promised in the following quote.

> דברים פרק ל' פסוק א-ה
> וְהָיָה כִי יָבֹאוּ עָלֶיךָ כָּל הַדְּבָרִים הָאֵלֶּה הַבְּרָכָה וְהַקְּלָלָה אֲשֶׁר נָתַתִּי לְפָנֶיךָ וַהֲשֵׁבֹתָ אֶל לְבָבֶךָ בְּכָל הַגּוֹיִם אֲשֶׁר הִדִּיחֲךָ ד' אֱלֹקיךָ שָׁמָּה: וְשַׁבְתָּ עַד ד' אֱלֹקיךָ וְשָׁמַעְתָּ בְקֹלוֹ כְּכֹל אֲשֶׁר אָנֹכִי מְצַוְּךָ הַיּוֹם אַתָּה וּבָנֶיךָ בְּכָל לְבָבְךָ וּבְכָל נַפְשֶׁךָ: וְשָׁב ד' אֱלֹקיךָ אֶת שְׁבוּתְךָ וְרִחֲמֶךָ וְשָׁב וְקִבֶּצְךָ מִכָּל הָעַמִּים אֲשֶׁר הֱפִיצְךָ ד' אֱלֹקיךָ שָׁמָּה: אִם יִהְיֶה נִדַּחֲךָ בִּקְצֵה הַשָּׁמָיִם מִשָּׁם יְקַבֶּצְךָ ד' אֱלֹקיךָ וּמִשָּׁם יִקָּחֶךָ: וֶהֱבִיאֲךָ ד' אֱלֹקיךָ אֶל הָאָרֶץ אֲשֶׁר יָרְשׁוּ אֲבֹתֶיךָ וִירִשְׁתָּהּ וְהֵיטִבְךָ וְהִרְבְּךָ מֵאֲבֹתֶיךָ:

---

26 Even the skeptics admit that it was "written" at least 2,300 years ago; the Greek translation was widely known by that time.

It will be that when all these things have come upon you, the blessing and the curse which I have placed before you, (then) you shall turn it over to your heart among all the nations where Hashem has dispersed you there. You shall return unto Hashem, your G-d, and listen to His voice as all that I command you today, you and your children with all your heart and all your nefesh. (Then) Hashem will return your captives and have mercy upon you. He will gather you from all the nations where He has scattered you there. If your dispersed will be in the end of the heavens, from there Hashem will gather you and from there He will take you. Hashem, your G-d, will bring you to the land which your forefathers inherited and you will inherit it. He will do good to you and multiply you more than your forefathers.

A LITTLE HISTORY

In order to be properly prepared for the next section, we need a little historical background. The first Beis Hamikdash, which was built by Shlomo haMelech, stood for four hundred and ten years. The *Shechinah* dwelt in that Beis Hamikdash and there was a constant sign of heavenly approval — a fire from Heaven that consumed the *korbanos*. During that period, there was still a *yetzer hara* for idolatry, and this was then the main sin of the Jewish people. They also transgressed other serious *aveiros*, including sins of immorality and murder, which constituted a full-fledged rebellion against Hashem's Torah. A mere eighteen years before the *churban*, Nevuchadnetzar, king of Bavel, conquered Yerushalayim and turned the land of Yehudah into a puppet state. He chose and set on the throne of Yehudah a member of the Jewish royal family, pillaged the treasuries, took some captives and laid a yearly tax on the land. That king of Yehudah (and a later one) rebelled against Nevuchadnetzar, who sent his armies to put down the rebellion. There was a siege which lasted about two-and-a-half years. Up until the beginning of the siege, life carried on somewhat normally in Eretz Yehudah. The Jews were not treated as slaves nor was their personal property taken. However, when the Babylonians finally broke through the wall of Yerushalayim, everything changed. There was a slaughter, and the city — with the Beis Hamikdash — was burnt. Almost all the remaining Jews were marched off to Bavel, beginning the period known to us as *galus Bavel* (the Babylonian exile). The Babylonians were not engaged in any slave trade. They didn't separate families in order to sell the youth into slavery. The language of Bavel was Aramaic, a sister language to Hebrew, with which we were quite familiar.

The Babylonian exile lasted for seventy years. During that time, Bavel was conquered by Persia. The Persian king Koresh gave permission to return to Eretz Yehudah and to rebuild the Beis Hamikdash, which was completed seventy years after the destruction of the first Beis Hamikdash. The group that returned to the Holy Land at that time was impoverished and constantly under threat of attack from their gentile neighbors in and around the land.

There was no particular wave of *teshuvah* at this point in history. Although we find the leaders of the era (such as *Daniel, Ezra and Nechemya*) confessing the sins of the people, the Jewish people were at a very low spiritual level, especially the ones who returned to Eretz Yisrael. There were quite a number of them that had even intermarried with the gentiles around.

BACK TO THE TIME OF THE CHURBAN

We were warned of the consequences of breaking the Torah in advance. We chose to ignore the warnings, and everything came true exactly as prescribed in the *parshah* called the *tochachah*. Pay careful attention to this excerpt from Ramban,[27] and see for yourself that all the details of both *churban Bayis Rishon* and *churban Bayis Sheini* were all predicted long in advance.

> **רמב"ן ויקרא פרק כו פסוק טז**
>
> ודע והבן כי האלות האלה ירמזו לגלות ראשון כי בבית הראשון היו כל דברי הברית הזאת הגלות והגאולה ממנו. שכן תראה בתוכחות שאמר ואם בחקתי תמאסו ואם את משפטי תגעל נפשכם. ואמר להפרכם את בריתי והזכיר בהם במות וחמנים וגלולים (פסוק ל), כי היו עובדי עבודת כוכבים ועושים כל הרעות. והוא שאמר (פסוק לא) והשימותי את מקדשיכם ולא אריח בריח ניחוחכם, יתרה בהם לסלק מהם מקדשו וקבול הקרבנות שהיו לרצון לו במקדש ההוא. והעונשים עליהם: חרב והיה רעה ודבר ורעב, וגלות בסוף כי כל זה היה שם כאשר בא בפירוש בספר ירמיהו (פרק ל"ב פסוק כ"ד).

---

27 There is another approach to understanding these two *parshiyos*, as found in *Abarbanel* and other commentaries. Based on those explanations, the Torah also foresaw the future clearly. However, for the sake of brevity, we have only quoted Ramban here.

Know and understand that these curses (in Bechukosai) hint to the first exile, for in the first Beis Hamikdash all the words of this covenant came true, the exile and the redemption from it. For so you will see in the (pesukim of) rebuke that it says, "If you loathe my statutes and repel my ordinances (which means a complete desertion of the Torah). And it (also) says, "To nullify my covenant (completely)." It mentions concerning them (those people) idolatrous worshipping places, sun idols and statues, for they were worshipping idols and doing all evil things. That is the meaning of the verse that says, "I will desolate your holy places (the Beis Hamikdash), and I will not smell your sweet smell." He warns them that He will remove the Beis Hamikdash from them and the acceptance of the sacrifices, which were pleasing to Him in that Mikdash. The punishments on them (on those sins) were the sword, wild animals, sickness, and exile in the end, as are explicitly spoken of in the book of Yirmiyahu.

ואמר בגלות (פסוקים ל"ד ל"ה) אז תרצה הארץ את שבתותיה וגו' כל ימי השמה תשבות את אשר לא שבתה. שהיו שנות הגלות כשנים אשר בטלו השמיטות. וכן אמר הכתוב בגלות ההוא (דברי הימים ב' פרק ל"ו פסוק כ"א) למלאת דבר ה' בפי ירמיהו עד רצתה הארץ את שבתותיה כל ימי השמה שבתה למלאת שבעים שנה. כן התרה בהם וכן הגיע אליהם, א"כ דבר ברור הוא שעל הגלות ההוא דיבר הכתוב:

Concerning the exile it says, "Then the land will appease for its Sabbatical years... All the years of its desolation it will rest, that which it did not rest (before)." For the years of the exile corresponded to the years in which they broke the shemittos. So it says concerning that exile (Chronicles II, chapter 36 verse 21), "To fulfill the word of Hashem through Yirmiyahu 'until the land appeased for its Sabbatical years, all the days of its desolation it rested, to complete seventy years.'" So He warned them, and so it came upon them. If so, it is clear that the verses (in Bechukosai) spoke about that exile.

והסתכל עוד בעניין הגאולה ממנו שאינו מבטיח רק שיזכור ברית אבות ובזכירת הארץ (פסוק מ"ב) לא שימחול עונם ויסלח חטאתם, ויוסיף אהבתם כקדם, ולא שיאסוף את נדחיהם. כי היה כן בעלותם מבבל, שלא שבו רק יהודה ובנימין והלוים עמהם מעט, ומקצת השבטים אשר גלו לבבל, ושבו בדלות, בעבדות מלכי פרס. וגם לא אמר שישובו בתשובה שלימה לפניו, רק שיתודו עונם ועון אבותם (פסוק מ'), ומצינו אנשי בית שני עושים כן כמו שהתודה דניאל (דניאל פרק ט' פסוק ה' ופסוק ח') חטאנו ועוינו והרשענו ומרדנו וסור ממצותיך וגו' למלכינו לשרינו ולאבותינו, וכתיב (שם פסוק ט"ז) כי בחטאינו ובעונות אבותינו ירושלים ועמך לחרפה. וכן נחמיה התודה (נחמיה פרק א' פסוק ה-י"א). ועזרא אמר (שם פרק ט' פסוק ל"ד) מלכינו שרינו כהנינו ואבותינו לא עשו תורתך, הרי כי כולם למדו מן התורה שיתודו עונם

> ועון אבותם. וכל אלה דברים ברורים בברית הזאת שהוא באמת ירמוז לגלות הראשון והגאולה ממנו:
>
> Consider further about the redemption from this exile. The Torah promises nothing more than that Hashem will remember the covenant and the land, not that He will forgive their iniquities, atone for their sins, continue to love them as before, and gather in their scattered people. So it was when they came up from Bavel, that only Yehudah and Binyamin and a little bit of the Levi'im returned with them, and a small part of the tribes that had been exiled to Bavel. They returned in poverty as servants to the kings of Persia. It also doesn't say that they would return to Hashem in a total teshuvah, but merely they would confess their sins and the sins of their fathers. We find that the men of the Second Temple did so. Daniel confessed, "We have sinned and rebelled and turned away from your mitzvos… our kings, our officials and our fathers." It is (also) written, "Because of our sins and the sins of our fathers, Yerushalayim and your people have been put to shame." Nechemiah did the same. Also Ezra said, "Our kings, our officials, our kohanim and our fathers did not keep Your Torah." You see that all of them learned from the Torah that they should confess their sins and the sins of their fathers. All these things make it very clear that this covenant truly hints to the first exile and the redemption from it.

THE HISTORY OF THE BAYIS SHEINI

Before we continue with the words of Ramban, we need to review briefly the history of *Bayis Sheini*.

The sins that the people of *Bayis Sheini* committed were very different than the sins of the *Bayis Rishon*. Whereas in *Bayis Rishon*, they transgressed the three cardinal sins of idolatry, immorality and murder, the people of the second Beis Hamikdash era were very devout, involved in learning Torah and performing acts of *chesed*. Their main sin was the constant infighting, politics, and causeless hatred that each group had for the other. The Gemara states so openly[28] (as quoted by Ramban).

---

28 *Yoma* 9b.

There was no *Shechinah* in the second Beis Hamikdash nor was there a heavenly fire to consume their sacrifices. In the second Beis Hamikdash, there was no idolatry. The Men of the Great Assembly, at the very beginning of that era, had fasted and prayed that the evil inclination to worship idols be removed. Their prayers were answered, and idolatry was no longer a temptation for our people.[29]

The second Beis Hamikdash was destroyed by Rome, which was considered very far away from Eretz Yisrael, in contrast to the first Beis Hamikdash, which was destroyed by nearby Bavel.[30] Whereas the Aramaic language of Bavel had been very familiar to the Jews, the tongue of the Romans was completely foreign to them.

The Romans overpowered Eretz Yisrael long before the *churban*. The Roman governors made life unbearable with excessive taxes, constant confiscations of property and other forms of oppression. Unlike Bavel, the Romans had a thriving slave trade, and they took away the youth from their families to sell them in ports throughout the Roman Empire.

While *galus Bavel* had lasted a mere seventy years, the *galus* put upon us by Rome, almost two thousand years ago, has not yet ended.

Now we return to the Ramban to see how the Torah foresaw all this history in advance.

> **רמב"ן שם**
>
> אבל הברית שבמשנה תורה ירמז לגלותנו זה ולגאולה שנגאל ממנו. כי הסתכלנו תחילה שלא נרמז שם קץ וקצב ולא הבטיח בגאולה רק תלה אותה בתשובה. ולא הזכיר בעבירות ההם שיעשו אשרים וחמנים ושיעבדו עבודת כוכבים כלל, אבל אמר (דברים פרק כ"ח פסוק ט"ו) 'והיה אם לא תשמע בקול ה' אלהיך לשמור לעשות את כל מצותיו וחקותיו'. אמר כי מפני שיעברו על קצת מצותיו שלא ישמרו ויעשו את כולן יענשו. שכך היה בבית שני כמו שאמרו (יומא ט:) 'בית ראשון מפני מה חרב? מפני עבודת כוכבים וגילוי עריות ושפיכות דמים. בית שני שאנו בקיאים בהם שהיו עוסקין בתורה ובגמילות חסדים מפני מה חרב? מפני שנאת חנם שהיתה ביניהם.' ולא הזכיר שם המקדש וריח ניחוח כאשר הזכיר כאן, שלא היתה האש יורדת ואוכלת הקרבנות בבית שני כמו שהעידו במסכת יומא שם (כא.):

---

29 Those Jews that bowed to the Greek idols did not do so out of a passion for idol worship, but only to find favor in the eyes of the Greeks.

30 Ancient Bavel is located in modern day Iraq, much closer to Israel than Rome.

But the covenant in Mishneh Torah (Devarim) hints to this galus of ours and to the redemption that we will be redeemed from it. For we first contemplated that it is not hinted there an end or time limit, nor did the Torah promise an (unconditional) redemption, but rather made it conditional on our repentance. Among the sins mentioned there it does not mention that they will make asheiros (trees that were worshipped) or sun altars, or that they would worship avodah zarah at all. But rather it says, "It will be, if you do not listen to the voice of Hashem, your G-d, to keep and do all His commands and statutes." It means that because they will transgress some of the mitzvos which they will not keep, they will be punished. So it was in the Bayis Sheini, as they (the chachamim) said (Yoma 9a), "Why was the first Beis Hamikdash destroyed? Because of idolatry, immorality and murder. The Bayis Sheini, about whom we know very well that they were involved in Torah learning and in the performance of kind deeds, why was it destroyed? Because of causeless hatred that was between them." It (also) does not mention the Mikdash and the sweet smell (of the sacrifices) as it mentions here (in Bechukosai), for the fire did not come down to consume the korbanos in the second Beis Hamikdash, as our Sages testified in Mesechta Yoma.

ואמר בקללות (דברים כח מט) "ישא ד' עליך גוי מרחוק מקצה הארץ כאשר ידאה הנשר." שבאו עליהם עם רומי הרחוקים מהם מאד. ואמר שם אל גוי אשר לא ידעת (שם פסוק לו) "גוי אשר לא תשמע לשונו" (שם פסוק מט) מפני רוב רחוקם מארצנו. ולא כן בדברי הברית הזאת, כי גלו לבבל ואשור שהם קרובים לארץ ונלחמים בהם תמיד ויחוס ישראל משם היה ויודעים לשונם כענין שנאמר (מ"ב יח כו) "דבר נא אל עבדיך ארמית כי שומעים אנחנו." וכן "והפיצך ד' בכל העמים מקצה הארץ" ועד קצה הארץ (דברים כח סד) הוא גלותנו היום שאנו מפוזרים מסוף העולם ועד סופו. ואמר (שם פסוק סח) "והשיבך ד' מצרים באניות" ובגלותנו זה היה שמילא טיטוס מהם ספינות וכן כתוב בספר הרומיים. וכן מה שאומר שם "בניך ובנותיך נתונים לעם אחר ועיניך רואות" (פסוק לב) "בנים ובנות תוליד ולא יהיו לך כי ילכו בשבי" (שם פסוק מא) איננו לגלות שגלו אבות ובנים רק השבי ההוא לבנים לבדם והאבות נשארים בארץ ולא נאמר כן בברית הראשון מפני שגלו גלות שלמה אבל בברית השני הזכיר כן שהיו הרומיים מושלים בארצנו ולוקחים הבנים והבנות כרצונם. וכן "ועבדת את אויבך אשר ישלחנו ד' בך ברעב ובצמא" (שם פסוק מח) היא עבדותנו שעבדנו הרומיים בארצנו ושריהם מושלים בארץ ומכבידים עלינו עול כבד ולוקחים גופינו וממונינו כאשר הוא ידוע בספרים.

In the curses (there in Devarim) it says, "Hashem will lift up over you a nation from far away, as the eagle[31] swoops," that the Romans who were

---

31 It is well known that the symbol of Roman legions was the eagle.

very far away came upon them. It further says (that Hashem will exile your king), "To a nation that you did not know (before). A nation whose language you do not understand." (All this) because they were so far away from our land. It was not so in this covenant (here in Bechukosai), for they were exiled to Bavel and to Ashur, which are very close to the land (of Israel). There were constant wars with them, Yisrael's lineage was from there, and they knew their language, as it says (when the Jewish representatives were speaking to the generals of Ashur), "Speak to your servants in Aramaic because we understand it." Also, (when it says), "Hashem will scatter you amongst all the nations, from the end of the earth to the end of the earth," that refers to our exile today, that we are dispersed from one end of the earth to the other. It says, "Hashem will return you to Mitzrayim in ships." that was in this galus, when Titus filled boats with them, as is recorded in the Book of the Romans. Also what is stated, "Your sons and daughters will be given to another nation and yours eyes will see (it)" and "Sons and daughter you will have, but they won't be for you, for they will go off in captivity." This does not refer to the (first) galus, where the fathers and sons went into galus (together), but rather to a captivity where the children alone were taken, and the fathers remained in the land. It doesn't say this by the first covenant because they were exiled a complete galus (all together). However, by the second covenant it mentions so, because the Romans ruled over our land and took their sons and daughters at will. Also (the verse), "You will serve your enemies, whom Hashem will send among you, in hunger and thirst," refers to our servitude that we served the Romans in our own land. Their officials ruled over us and placed a heavy yoke upon us, taking our bodies and our money, as is well known in (many) books.

ועוד ראיה שאמר (שם פרק כ"ח פסוק ל"ו) יולך ד' אותך ואת מלכך אשר תקים עליך אל גוי אשר לא ידעת אתה ואבותיך, כי הלך אגריפס המלך בסוף בית שני לרומי ועל הליכתו שם נחרב הבית, ולא אמר הכתוב "המלך אשר ימלוך עליך", אבל אמר "מלכך אשר תקים", רמז לנו יתברך שלא היה ראוי למלוך ואסור היה להיות מלך על ישראל מדין תורה, אבל הקימו עליהם הוא ואבותיו שלא כדת, כמו שהוזכר זה במסכת סוטה (מא.). וכל אלה רמזים כאלו יזכירו בפירוש ענין גלותנו זה:

And another proof (that the tochachah in Devarim refers to the second Beis Hamikdash) is what is says, "Hashem will take you and your king that you will put upon you to a nation that you and your forefathers did not know (before)." King Agrippas went to Rome at the end of the second bayis, and as a result of his going there the Beis Hamikdash was destroyed. The pasuk did not say, "The king that will reign over you," but rather, "The king that you will appoint," because Hashem Yisborach hints to us that he was not fit to reign and it was forbidden for him to be a king over Yisrael by the law of the Torah, but they had put him and his forefathers up not in accordance with the law, as it is mentioned in Mesechta Sotah. All these hints are as if they mention explicitly this galus of ours.

והגאולה בברית ההיא השנית גאולה שלמה מעולה על כלם. אמר (דברים ל א) והיה כי יבאו עליך כל הדברים האלה הברכה והקללה וגו', והבטיח (שם פסוק ה) והטיבך והרבך מאבותיך, שהיא הבטחה לכל שבטי ישראל לא לשתית העם. ושם הבטיח שיכרת ויכלה המגלים אותנו שנאמר (שם פסוק ז) ונתן ד' אלקיך את כל האלות האלה על אויביך ועל שונאיך אשר רדפוך. והנה אויביך ושונאיך רמז לשתי האומות אשר ירדפו תמיד אחרינו: ואלה דברים יבטיחו בגאולה העתידה הבטחה שלמה יותר מכל חזיונות דניאל.

And the redemption mentioned in this second covenant will be a complete redemption for everyone (the entire people). It says, "When all these things will come upon you, the blessing and the curse (at the end of the punishments)..." Then it promises, "He will do good to you and multiply you more than your forefathers." This is a promise for all the tribes of Yisrael (including the ten lost tribes), not just for a sixth of the people (Yehudah and Binyomin). (And since this didn't happen by the first redemption, it means that it refers to the second, which we still await). There it promises us that Hashem will cut off and make an end of the ones who sent us into exile, as it says, "Hashem will put all these curses on your enemies and those that hate you, who have pursued you." "Your enemies and those that hate you" hint to the two nations that constantly pursue us (the Christians and the Moslems). These things reassure us of the future redemption with a complete promise more than all the visions of Daniel.

וכן מה שאמר בכאן (בפסוק לב) ושממו עליה אויביכם, היא בשורה טובה מבשרת בכל הגליות שאין ארצנו מקבלת את אויבינו. וגם זו ראיה גדולה והבטחה לנו כי לא תמצא בכל הישוב ארץ אשר היא טובה ורחבה ואשר היתה נושבת מעולם והיא חרבה כמוה. כי מאז יצאנו ממנה לא קבלה אומה ולשון וכולם משתדלים להושיבה ואין לאל ידם:

Also what it says here (in Bechukosai), "Your enemies will be desolate upon it (the land)": This is a promise of good news to us, which informs us that in all the exiles our land will never receive our enemies. This, too, is a great proof (of the truth of the Torah) and a promise to us. You shall not find

> anywhere in the civilized world a land which is better and broader than it, and which was always settled, which is as destroyed as it is. From the time that we left it, it did not accept any nation or tongue. All of them endeavor to settle it, but are powerless to do so.
>
> והנה הברית הראשונה אשר בפרשה הזאת הקב"ה כרת אותה, כי כן היה שמו הגדול עמנו בבית הראשון. והברית השנית שבפרשה והיה כי תבא מפי משה רמז לסילוקו שכינתו לגמרי שלא היה בבית שני רק כבוד שמו וכו'
>
> Behold, Hakadosh Baruch Hu Himself made the first covenant which is in this parshah, for so it was that His great name was with us in the first bayis. But the second covenant in parshas Ki Savo was said through Moshe. That was a hint to the complete removal of the Shechinah, which was not in the second bayis, but merely the honor of His name (was there).

The following is a review, in outline form, of some of the differences that Ramban points out between the *tochachah* in *parshas Bechukosai* and the *tochachah* in *parshas Ki Savo*. The Ramban's conclusion, as we have already shown at length, is that the *tochachah* in *B'chukosei* is a description of *churban Bayis Rishon* and the *tochachah* in *Ki Savo* is an accurate description of *churban Bayis Sheini*.

תוכחה - דברים פרק כ"ח	תוכחה - ויקרא פרק כ"ו
א) מפי משה כי לא היה שכינה בבית שני Moshe said the curses, because there was no *Shechinah* in the *Bayis Sheini*	א) הקב"ה כרת את הברית הזאת בעצמו Hashem speaks in first person

ב) "ואם בחקתי תמאסו ואם את משפטי תגעל נפשכם ..... להפרכם את בריתי" [כי היו עובדי ע"ז ועושים כל הרעות] The *pasuk* indicates a complete rejection of Torah	ב) "לשמר לעשות את כל מצותיו" [מפני שיעברו על קצת מצותיו שלא ישמרו ויעשו את כולן יענשו] The *pasuk* indicates that they will transgress some of the mitzvos, but not all
ג) במות חמנים וגלולים There was *avodah zarah* in the First Temple	ג) אין זכר מע"ז No mention of *avodah zarah*
ד) "והשמתי את מקדשיכם ולא אריח בריח ניחוחכם" יתרה בהם לסלק מהם מקדשו וקבול הקרבנות שהיו לרצון לו במקדש ההוא Removal of Divine acceptance of *korbanos*	ד) אין זכר מהמקדש והקרבנות No mention of the Mikdash, *korbanos*
ה) חרב וחיה רעה ודבר ורעב וגלות בסוף [ואין שום זכר מעבדות] No servitude in our land before the *galus*	ה) סדר אחר: עבדות קודם "ישא ד' אליך גוי מרחוק" ואין זכר מחיה רעה Servitude in our land before the *galus*

ו) לא נרמז קץ וקצב [ואף פרשת הגאולה נכתב ברחוק מן התוכחה] רק תלה אותה בתשובה No set time, redemption depends on *teshuvah*	ו) קצבה לשנות הגלות ע' שנים כנגד ע' שנות השמיטות שבטלו Fixed time for the exile corresponding to *shemittos* they didn't keep
ז) גאולה שלמה מעולה בקבוץ נדחים וגם הבטיח בתשובה שלמה Complete redemption, full *teshuvah*	ז) אינו מבטיח בגאולה ובקבוץ נדחים רק שיזכור ברית אבות ובזכירת הארץ. גם לא הבטיח בתשובה שלמה רק שיתודו עונם No ingathering of exiles, no complete *teshuvah*
ח) "ישא ד' עליך גוי מרחוק מקצה הארץ גוי אשר לאז תשמע לשונו" Enemy (Rome) was from far away	ח) לא הזכיר רחוק כי בבל קרוב לארצנו ומבינים שפתם Enemy from far not mentioned. Bavel was close
ט) "והפיצך ד' בכל העמים מקצה הארץ ועד קצה הארץ" Will be scattered from one end of world to other	ט) "ואתכם אזרה בגוים" ולא מקצה הארץ ועד קצה הארץ Will be scattered, but not throughout the world

י) אין זכר מזה No mention of slave boats	י) "והשיבך ד' מצרים באניות." שמילא טיטוס מהם ספינות Titus filled boats to send to slave markets
כ) גלו גלות שלמה כולם ביחד אבות ובנים Families exiled all together	כ) "בניך ובנותיך נתונות לעם אחר ועיניך רואות וכלות עליהם" ... "בנים ובנות תוליד ולא יהיו לך כי ילכו בשבי" [וזה איננו הגלות שגלו אבות ובנים] Children taken away to be sold as slaves
ל) אין זכר מזה No mention of king taken into exile	ל) "יולך ד' אותך ואת מלכך אשר תקים עליך אל גוי אשר לא ידעת אתה ואבותיך" [הליכת אגריפס לרומי שגרם לחורבן הבית] King will go to the enemy land (resulting in *churban*)
מ) חזרה רק למקצת העם Small percentage of the people will return	מ) "והטיבך והרבך מאבותיך" More numerous and better than ever by the Geula
נ) אין זכר מזה No mention of destroying the enemies	נ) הבטיח שיכלה ויכרית המגלים אותנו Total destruction of our enemies by redemption

He Knows in Advance

WE AREN'T THE ONLY GOOD FARMERS

Let us return to one of the issues that Ramban mentioned. Rashi had already pointed out that as long as the Jewish people are not living in Eretz Yisrael, the land would not yield its fruits to any strangers.

> **רש"י ויקרא פרק כו פסוק לב**
>
> "והשמתי אני את הארץ". זו מדה טובה לישראל שלא ימצאו האויבים נחת רוח בארצם שתהא שוממה מיושביה
>
> *"I will make the land desolate." This is a good measure for Yisrael, that their enemies will never have any satisfaction from their land as long as it is deserted by its (true) inhabitants.*

Ramban, at the end of his life, was forced to flee Spain, and came to Eretz Yisrael. He personally saw the fulfillment of this prophecy, and he declared that this was a great additional proof to us of the truth of the Torah. We repeat these few lines because of their significance.

> **רמב"ן ויקרא פרק כו פסוק טז (באמצע דבריו)**
>
> וכן מה שאמר בכאן (בפסוק לב) "ושממו עליה אויביכם," היא בשורה טובה מבשרת בכל הגליות שאין ארצנו מקבלת את אויבינו. וגם זו ראיה גדולה והבטחה לנו כי לא תמצא בכל הישוב ארץ אשר היא טובה ורחבה ואשר היתה נושבת מעולם והיא חרבה כמוה כי מאז יצאנו ממנה לא קבלה אומה ולשון וכולם משתדלים להושיבה ואין לאל ידם:
>
> *Also what it says here (in Bechukosai), "Your enemies will we desolate upon it (the land)," is a promise of good news to us, which informs us that in all the exiles our land will never receive our enemies. This, too, is a great proof (of the truth of the Torah) and a promise to us. You shall not find anywhere in the civilized world a land which is better and broader than it, and which was always settled, which is as ruined as it is. From the time that we left it, it did not accept any nation or tongue. All of them endeavor to settle it, but are powerless to do so.*

This is an astounding prediction in the Torah. Jews are certainly not the only good farmers in the world, and the Land of Israel has always been coveted. It was conquered by various nations numerous times throughout the centuries, but no one could ever get the land to produce.

Who (but the Creator) could have known that no strangers would ever derive benefit from the land? If a luscious land is left untilled, it should become overgrown, like a jungle, not desolate like a desert.

However, the Ramban saw only the fulfillment of the first half of this prophecy — the land would indeed lie in waste. We, in our time, are witness to the second half. The promise implied that as long as our enemies are the main inhabitants of the land, it will not yield its produce to them. However, as soon as large numbers of Jews return, the land will once again become fertile and luscious. This is precisely what has transpired over the last hundred years. Today, Eretz Yisrael has vast orchards and fields with crops of grain, fruit and vegetables.[32] These words, written over three thousand years ago, have come true to the letter.

A SURPRISING OMISSION

Following in the footsteps of Ramban, the author of a brilliant *sefer*, *Doros Harishonim*, shows us two more important differences between the two portions of the *tochachah*.

During the entire era of the First Temple, the most widespread sin was the worship of idols. As previously mentioned, at the very beginning of the second Beis Hamikdash, the *Anshei K'neses Hag'dolah* (Men of the Great Assembly) prayed to Hashem to remove the *yetzer hara* for idol worship. Hashem accepted their *tefillos*, and the temptation for idol worship was removed.

In about a dozen places, where the Torah forewarns us about straying from the *derech Hashem*, it singles out the *aveirah* of *avodah zarah*. Indeed, the sin most often mentioned in the entire Tanach is the sin of idol worship. We cite just two examples of many:

> דברים פרק ח פסוק יט-כ
> והיה אם שכח תשכח את ד' אלקיך והלכת אחרי אלהים אחרים ועבדתם והשתחוית להם העדתי בכם היום כי אבד תאבדון: כגוים אשר ד' מאביד מפניכם כן תאבדון עקב לא תשמעון בקול ד' אלקיכם:

---

32 Wikipedia states: **Agriculture in Israel** is a highly developed industry: Israel is a major exporter of fresh produce, etc... Israel produces 95% of its own food requirements.

> It shall come to be that if you forget Hashem, your G-d, and go after other gods, serve them and bow to them, I warn you today that you shall perish. Just as the nations that Hashem destroyed before you, so shall you perish, because you did not listen to the voice of Hashem, your G-d.

> דברים פרק יא פסוק טז-יז
> השמרו לכם פן יפתה לבבכם וסרתם ועבדתם אלהים אחרים והשתחויתם להם: וחרה אף ד' בכם ועצר את השמים ולא יהיה מטר והאדמה לא תתן את יבולה ואבדתם מהרה מעל הארץ הטבה אשר ד' נתן לכם:
>
> Guard yourself, lest your heart be enticed and you turn aside and worship other gods and bow to them. Hashem's anger will be kindled against you. He will close up the heavens and there will be no rain. The ground will not yield its produce. You shall perish quickly from upon the good land which Hashem has given you.

There is one *parshah* which is a notable exception. The longest, most detailed warning in the whole Torah is the *tochachah* in *parshas Ki Savo*. In all fifty-five *pesukim*, there is not the slightest mention of *avodah zarah*. This can be understood only in light of the Ramban's insight, that this *parshah* refers to the second Beis Hamikdash. By that time, there was no longer any *avodah zarah*. Politics and causeless hatred were their sins, but not idol worship. Once again, the Torah foresaw the future, precisely as it would occur.

THE SAMARITANS

There is another astounding prediction pointed out by the author of *Doros Harishonim*. In a *pasuk* in *Ki Savo* we learn:

> דברים פרק כח פסוק מג-מד
> הגר אשר בקרבך יעלה עליך מעלה מעלה ואתה תרד מטה מטה: הוא ילוך ואתה לא תלונו הוא יהיה לראש ואתה תהיה לזנב:
>
> The convert that is among you will rise over you higher and higher, and you will go down lower and lower. He will lend you (money) and you will not lend him. He will be the head and you will be the tail.

It is likely that this mysterious sounding verse would have made no sense to someone living during the era of the first Beis Hamikdash. However, in the era of *Bayis Sheini*, this verse came true, and needed no explanation. There were actually two circumstances in which the convert went "higher and higher" and we, the Jewish people, went "lower and lower." The first concerns the *Kusim*, and the second concerns Herod, king of Yehudah.[33]

The *Kusim* (otherwise known as *Shomronim* or Samaritans) were sworn enemies of the Jews. They were brought into Eretz Yisrael at the time that the ten Northern tribes of *Yisrael* were exiled. As related in Tanach,[34] they converted to Judaism out of fear of punishment from Hashem. When *Bnei Yisrael* returned some two hundred years after the *Kusim* had come, they greatly resented the Jewish presence. Any Jew who passed through their territory was in danger of being murdered. The *Beis Din* was not strong enough to exert power over them, and they caused many troubles for the Jewish people. They were extremely wealthy. Early in the Second Temple era, the country was under the rule of the Egyptian kings. The *kohen gadol* was lax in raising the taxes that were due to be delivered to the king. He had a very crafty but wicked nephew, named Yosef ben Tovia. The nephew offered to raise the taxes. He did so by going to the *Kusim*, with whom he was very friendly, and borrowing an enormous sum of money from them. He went to Egypt, offered to pay the king in advance for the taxes, and asked for an army to help him raise the taxes back from the people. He came back to Eretz Yisrael with an army of 3,000 soldiers, terrorized the people by threatening to kill them if they didn't pay him seven times the amount formerly paid. He literally took over, with the help of his loan from the *Kusim*. This was the beginning of the *misyavnim* (Hellenizers), which eventually led to the ruin of the country.

HEROD, KING OF JUDAH

After the war of Chanukah, the righteous *Chashmonaim*, who had led the battle, took the throne of Yehudah for themselves. Although the

---

33 As per Josephus, quoted in *Doros Harishonim*, by Rabbi Isaac Halevi Rabinowitz, volume *Tekufas Hamikra*, p. 110.

34 *Melachim II*, chapter 17.

Chashmonaim were very pious, their descendants eventually became corrupt, allying themselves with the ruthless *Tzedukim*. They did many things which were not approved of by the Torah. One such thing was that when Yochanan Horkonos haMelech conquered Edom, he forced the Edomites to convert and become *gerim*. This was done against the will of the *chachamim*.

Eventually, one of these *gerim*, Antipater, manipulated his way to gain control of the land of Yehudah. His son, *Hurdos* (Herod), charmed Rome into making him king of Yehudah. His reign was one of terror. Although he built many cities in Eretz Yisrael, they were all-gentile cities. For the Jews he did nothing.[35] He actually made them feel like foreigners in their own land. He taxed them exceedingly, and they always owed him money. Hurdos' dynasty lasted one hundred and three years, up until the *churban* of the Beis Hamikdash. He and his descendants went "higher and higher," while the Jews went "lower and lower." He lent them money, but never the other way around — exactly as predicted by the Torah in the portion about the Second Temple that the convert among us would go higher and higher, while we would go lower and lower.

(מספר דורות הראשונים) (חלק תקופת המקרא פרק כא-כב)

	הגר אשר בקרבך יעלה עליך מעלה מעלה.
	"על אנטיפטר ובניו והורדוס ובניו."
	"The convert among you will go higher and higher over you."
אין זכר מזה בפרשת בחקתי	"גם על הכותים נאמרו הדברים. כולם היו מלוים כסף הרבה ככתוב הוא ילוך ואתה לא תלונו."
No mention of converts here	"Also the wealthy *Kusim* lent money to the Jewish people."

---

35 All the cities that he built, with money extorted from the Jews, were exclusively gentile cities. After he murdered the majority of the *chachamim*, he felt a sense of remorse and the sage, Bava ben Buta, advised him to build a new Beis Hamikdash, to replace the old one, which was very run down.

ONE MORE ASTOUNDING PIECE OF FOREKNOWLEDGE

As we have already seen, the Ramban tells us that the *tochachah* in *Sefer Vayikra* is a prediction of the events at the time of the destruction of *Bayis Rishon*. At the end of that passage, there are a number of verses that seem to be in an incorrect order. Here are the *pesukim*:

> ויקרא פרק כו פסוק מב-מד
>
> וזכרתי את בריתי יעקוב ואף את בריתי יצחק ואף את בריתי אברהם אזכר והארץ אזכר: והארץ תעזב מהם ותרץ את שבתתיה בהשמה מהם והם ירצו את עונם יען וביען במשפטי מאסו ואת חקתי געלה נפשם: ואף גם זאת בהיותם בארץ איביהם לא מאסתים ולא געלתים לכלתם להפר בריתי אתם כי אני ד' אלקיהם: וזכרתי להם ברית ראשנים אשר הוצאתי אתם מארץ מצרים לעיני הגוים להיות להם לאלקים אני ד':

> *I will remember my covenant with Yaakov, also my covenant with Yitzchak, and also my covenant with Avraham. The land will (still) be deserted by them and appease for its Shabbos years (shemittah, yovel) while it is desolate from them. They will atone for their sins because they loathed my judgments and rejected my statutes. With all of this, while they are (still) in the land of their enemies, I will not loath them or reject them to destroy them, to nullify my covenant with them, for I am Hashem, their G-d. I will remember for them the covenant with the first ones whom I took out of Egypt, before the eyes of the nations, to be for them for Elokim, I am Hashem.*

In the first of these verses, the Torah tells us that Hashem will remember His covenant with the *Avos*. That seems to predict the end of the exile. Then the *pasuk* reverts back to the time of exile, and stresses that the land must appease for its *shemittah/yovel* years that were not properly kept.[36] Finally, the *pasuk* returns to speak about Hashem remembering His covenant with *Bnei Yisrael*, whom He took out of Mitzrayim. That obviously refers to the redemption, when Hashem will bring back the *Yidden* out of *galus* once again, just as He did when He took them out of Egypt. It would seem that the first of these four verses should be

---

36 Rashi tells us that the seventy-year exile corresponded to seventy Sabbatical years that were not observed properly.

together with the last. What is the meaning of this strange order? In order to appreciate the answer to this question, we need to review a bit of the history leading up to and following the destruction of the first Beis Hamikdash.

The Torah made it clear that the *galus* years, when the land will be deserted, are an atonement for the Sabbatical years that they did not properly observe.

> ויקרא פרק כו פסוק לד - לה
>
> אז תרצה הארץ את שבתתיה כל ימי השמה ואתם בארץ איביכם אז תשבת הארץ והרצת את שבתתיה: כל ימי השמה תשבת את אשר לא שבתה בשבתתיכם בשבתכם עליה:
>
> *Then the land will appease for its Sabbatical years, while you are in the land of your enemies. Then the land will rest and appease for the Shabbasos. All the days of its desolation it shall rest, that which you did not rest in your Sabbatical years while you lived upon it.*

Also in *Divrei Hayamim* it says that the years of *galus Bavel* corresponded to the years when they did not keep the *shemittah* and *yovel* properly.

> דברי הימים ב פרק לו פסוק כ
>
> עד רצתה הארץ את שבתותיה כל ימי השמה שבתה למלאות שבעים שנה:
>
> *Until the land appeased for its Shabbos years. All the days of its desolation it rested, to complete seventy years.*

Nevuchadnetzar became king of Bavel nineteen years before he destroyed the first Beis Hamikdash. The following year, he conquered the Jewish state, Yehudah. Hence, Yehudah was already under Bavel's rule eighteen years before the Temple was destroyed.

Fifty-one years after *churban Bais Hamikdash*, Bavel was defeated by Persia and Mead, under the rule of King Daryavesh. The following year, Daryavesh died, and his son-in-law, Koresh, king of Persia took the throne. Koresh proclaimed that anyone of *Bnei Yisrael* who wanted to cross over the Euphrates River, return to Eretz Yisrael, and rebuild the Beis Hamikdash could do so. This was exactly seventy years after Bavel had first conquered Yehudah. It was the time that the *geulah* was expected, based on the prophecy in *Sefer Yirmiyahu*.

> **ירמיהו פרק כט פסוק י**
> כי כה אמר ד' כי לפי מלאת לבבל שבעים שנה אפקד אתכם והקמתי עליכם את דברי הטוב להשיב אתכם אל המקום הזה:
>
> For so said Hashem, "When seventy years of Bavel are completed I will remember you and fulfill for you My good words, to return you to this place."

A small group went and began the work of rebuilding. They fully believed that they would be able to reestablish the Jewish state and rebuild the Temple, based on the promise quoted above. Sometime later, Koresh retracted his permission, and subsequently died. Achashverosh took the throne, Haman rose to power, and the story of Purim took place. There was a threat of annihilation on the Jewish people, but it was averted, as we read in the *Megillah*.

All this was a great shock to the people, who thought that the time for the redemption had already come and passed. Even the great Daniel was under that impression.

When Daniel *davened* to understand why the *geulah* had not yet come, he was told that the redemption would come, not seventy years after the initial conquest, but rather seventy years after the *churban* of Yerushalayim.

> **דניאל פרק ט פסוק ב**
> בשנת אחת למלכו אני דניאל בינתי בספרים מספר השנים אשר היה דבר ד' אל ירמיה הנביא למלאות לחרבות ירושלם שבעים שנה:
>
> In the first year of his (Koresh's) reign, I, Daniel, understood the number of years that were in the words of Hashem to Yirmiyahu (to mean): to complete from the destruction of Yerushalayim seventy years.

There is a discrepancy of eighteen years between the two prophecies. Now the question remained as to what was meant by the prophecy in *Yirmiyahu*. The Gemara discusses these two prophecies that seem to be in contradiction,[37] yet answers that there is no contradiction at all. The verse in *Yirmiyahu* did not say that there would be a full *geulah*. It merely said that there would be a remembrance. "I will remember you." The mere fact that Koresh allowed the return to Eretz Yisrael and the first steps of building of the Beis Hamikdash was an indication of being remembered by Hashem. After all, this was the first time since the *churban* that there was any Jewish presence at all in Eretz Yisrael. However, the ultimate redemption would come eighteen years later, which would be seventy years after the destruction of Yerushalayim. That is precisely what happened: Exactly seventy years after the *churban*, Daryavesh the Second allowed the Beis Hamikdash to be rebuilt.

Now we can see that the verses of the *Chumash* are in perfect order, for this entire period of history is hinted to exactly in the order in which it took place. First, there will be a remembering of the *Avos*: Koresh will allow a return to the land. You will think that the *geulah* has come, but it is not yet to be. "The land must still be deserted by them, in order to atone for the Sabbatical years." Then will come a threat of annihilation by Haman, but I won't allow it to happen. After that, I will bring the people out of exile, just as I did from Mitzrayim. The Torah foresaw all the events, and alluded to them exactly in the order on which they took place.

Everything we have said here is stated in the commentary of the Ramban in just a few short words.

> רמב"ן ויקרא פרק כו פסוק מג
>
> ופירוש והארץ תעזב מהם כי גם אחרי הזכירה תעזב מהם. רמז כי אחרי פקידת כורש נעזבה מהם ורצתה השמיטות עד אחרי תשע עשרה שנה שנבנה הבית... כל הקורות אותם רמוזות בפרשה הזאת:
>
> What is meant by "the land will be deserted" is that even after the remembrance it shall still remain deserted. For after the proclamation of Koresh it still remained deserted from them, while the land atoned for its Sabbatical years, until the nineteenth year when the Beis Hamikdash was rebuilt... All that happened to them is hinted in this parshah.

---

37 *Megillah* 12a.

NOT FINISHED YET

Truthfully, we have only scratched the surface of the astounding things our Torah predicts and have all come true. However, since we need to proceed, we will give just one more.

When the Romans finally overpowered the state of Yehudah and destroyed the Beis Hamikdash, they wanted revenge. The long, protracted war had cost them tremendous casualties and great expense. It was a terrible insult to the Roman empire that a small country should resist them for so long. In retaliation, they made decrees upon the Jewish people that were designed to crush the people both physically and spiritually. By the time sixty years had passed since the *churban*, the people could no longer bear the suffering. Under the leadership of Bar Kochba, they raised an army of four hundred thousand and chased the Romans out of Eretz Yisrael. Bar Kochba set up an independent kingdom which lasted a mere two-and-a-half years. Rome came back, conquering one town at a time, starting from the North in Galil. Eventually, they reached Yerushalayim, and Bar Kochba and his men had to flee. They went to a very well-fortified city which was located on a hilltop, the city of Beitar. After a long siege, the Romans finally penetrated the city and a massive slaughter ensued. They were bent on revenge. They decreed that the bodies of the slain were not allowed to be buried. Let us hear the story from the words of the *Talmud Yerushalmi*.

> **תלמוד ירושלמי פרק ד הלכה ה**
>
> כרם גדול היה לאדריינוס הרשע שמונה עשר מיל על שמונה עשר מיל כמן טיבריא לציפורי והקיפו גדר מהרוגי ביתר מלא קומה ופישוט ידים ולא גזר עליהם שיקברו עד שעמד מלך אחר וגזר עליהם שיקברו.
>
> Adraryanus[38] the wicked had a vineyard that was eighteen mil[39] by eighteen mil, like the distance from Tiberias to Tzipori. He surrounded it with a fence made from the slain of Beitar. They (were pressed together) full height, with arms stretched up. He never decreed that they may be buried, until another king arose and decreed upon them to be buried.

---

38 This was Hadrian, Emperor of Rome from 3877–3898 (117–138 C.E.)

39 A *mil* is two thousand *amos*, over half-a-mile in length.

I do not know if there is another such incident in recorded history. The Sages recorded a miracle that happened in connection with this. All the years that the slain were not allowed to be buried, their bodies did not decay. Our people have preserved this memory in the fourth blessing of the Grace after Meals, in which we thank Hashem for his benevolence. This is what our Sages have to say about this:

> מסכת ברכות דף מח עמוד ב
>
> הטוב והמטיב ביבנה תקנוה כנגד הרוגי ביתר. דאמר רב מתנא: אותו היום שניתנו הרוגי ביתר לקבורה תקנו ביבנה הטוב והמטיב, הטוב שלא הסריחו, והמטיב שניתנו לקבורה.
>
> *The blessing of Ha-tov v'ha-meitiv was instituted in Yavneh about the slain of Beitar. Rav Masneh said, "That day that the slain of Beitar were allowed to be buried, they instituted in Yavneh the blessing of Ha-tov V'ha-meitiv. Ha-tov that they didn't decay, V'ha-meitiv that they were (finally) allowed to be buried."*

This odd historical incident was clearly predicted in our Torah long before it took place:

> דברים כח פסוק כו
>
> וְהָיְתָה נִבְלָתְךָ לְמַאֲכָל לְכָל־עוֹף הַשָּׁמַיִם וּלְבֶהֱמַת הָאָרֶץ וְאֵין מַחֲרִיד:

IN CONCLUSION: YOU BE THE JUDGE

Can you imagine the Jewish people accepting a Torah from Moshe Rabbeinu if it had not all happened as described in that Torah? Could they have swallowed the stories of the ten *makkos*, the splitting of the Red Sea, the falling of *mann*, and *ma'amad Har Sinai* if they had not actually taken place?

Alternatively, could someone in a later era convince the entire nation to think that their forefathers had always had this Torah, until some time in history when it was completely forgotten? Wouldn't the Jewish people surely have known that they were hearing it now for the first time? Did that same someone hypnotize them to forget that he ever existed? History has never recorded such a person or such an event.

How could the scientific knowledge revealed in the Torah have been known to anyone in that time, if not through Divine Revelation? Could all the predictions of the future mentioned above have been merely lucky guesses? You be the judge. If indeed, your conclusion concurs with ours, then this Torah of ours is indeed the *d'var Hashem*. Now you have joined the millions of *Yidden* of the last three thousand years plus, who believed with every fiber of their being in everything we have said here.

In the next parts of this book, we hope to clarify other matters of *emunah* in similar fashion. We will endeavor to show how we can see Hashem's signature everywhere we look in the natural world; that His presence is most obvious, if we only open our minds and hearts. In the meanwhile, give careful consideration to all you have read here. May the thoughts presented here so far penetrate your very being, and give you the conviction and confidence that the Torah of your forefathers is indeed the absolute truth. אמן

PART THREE

THE CREATOR'S SIGNATURE IS EVERYWHERE

CHAPTER TWELVE

The Awesome Creator

In Part One of this *emunah* program, we have tried to make crystal clear that Torah is *min haShamayim*. If so, we don't really need to be introduced to our Creator. After all, He spoke to us "face to face" on Har Sinai. However, just knowing that He exists is not enough for us. We need to be aware of Hashem's presence at all times. For this we need to go to the next level.

A WALL OF EMUNAH

Nothing could be more fundamental to us than belief in the Creator. For this belief in Hashem (and His Torah) we have spilt rivers of blood and shed oceans of tears. Often, we were promised glorious benefits if we would just exchange our faith for another. Seldom did any Jew accept the offer. Time and time again we refused, often at cost of our lives. The Midrash tells us,[40] "[When people ask us], Why are you going out to be stoned? [we answer], 'Because I gave my son a *bris*.' Why are you going out to be burned? 'Because I kept the Shabbos.' Why are you going to be executed? 'Because I ate matzah.' Why are

---

Vayikra Rabbah 32:1.

you going to be beaten with a whip? 'Because I took a *lulav*'; 'Because I put on *tefillin*'; 'Because I put on *t'cheiles*'; 'Because I did the will of my Father in Heaven.'"

Almost invariably, our people refused to comply. Their *emunah* in Hashem and His Torah was like an iron wall. As *Klal Yisrael* declares in *Shir Hashirim*, "I am a wall" (in my *emunah*).[41] This clarity and confidence is what we hope to duplicate in ourselves.

As we said earlier, just agreeing to be a *ma'amin* by signing on the dotted line, as when a person signs a contract, is very superficial *emunah*. Belief should be equivalent to "knowing," without a doubt or any second thoughts. Once again, we bring the following quotation, where the *Sefer Hachinuch* explains the mitzvah of *"Anochi Hashem Elokecha."* He teaches us that belief in the existence of the Creator must be so clear that we realize there is simply no other possibility.

> ספר החינוך מצוה כה (משרשי המצוה)
>
> שורש מצוה זו אין צריך ביאור. ידוע הדבר ונגלה לכל כי האמונה הזו יסוד הדת ואשר לא יאמין בזה כופר בעיקר ואין לו חלק וזכות עם ישראל. וענין האמונה הוא שיקבע בנפשו שהאמת כן ושאי אפשר בחילוף זה בשום פנים ואם ישאל עליו ישיב לכל שואל שזה יאמין לבו ולא יודה בחילוף זה אפילו יאמרו להרגו.
>
> *The root of this mitzvah requires no clarification. It is well known and revealed to all that this belief is the foundation of our law. Whoever does not believe in this denies the most fundamental principal, and has no share or merit with the Jewish people. The idea of this emunah is that one should affix in his nefesh that this is the truth, and that anything to the contrary is absolutely impossible. Should he be asked about this, he will respond to any questioner that this is what his heart believes, and he would never admit to the contrary, even if they say they will murder him.*

Perhaps you think that such strong conviction is difficult to achieve. Truthfully, it is much simpler than you think.

---

41 *Shir Hashirim*, 8:10.

CHAPTER THIRTEEN

Know Who and What You Are Up Against

After we endeavor to bring the reality of Hashem's existence into our lives, we will need to deal with the prevailing theory that denies the existence of a Creator, and with their claim that their contentions have been proved. That will come later. There is, however, one thing we must bear in mind about these theories while we discuss *niflaos haBorei*. The proponents of the Big Bang and the theory of evolution say unequivocally that everything in the universe came to be with no intelligence behind it all.[42] It is only through totally unguided processes that all the complexities of nature came to be. When we finish our discussion of the natural world you will need to ask yourself, "Does common sense allow you to even entertain the idea that all this came about without any intelligence behind it? Does this not go against your *seichel*?" Bear this in mind, because it is the key to this issue.

---

42 Later we will discuss those that endeavor to make a synthesis of creation and evolution.

THREE THOUSAND YEARS OF "BEREISHIS"

Klal Yisrael has always remained steadfast in their belief that the Creator made the world during the six days of *Bereishis* — *yesh ma'ayin* (something from nothing). We maintain all the following: that creation did not occur through any natural processes, but was totally supernatural. Before that, there was nothing except for the Creator Himself. After the six days of creation, everything had already come into existence: all the animals, plants and even humans. Then came Shabbos,⁴³ when the world began to function according to what we call "the laws of nature." The supernatural era was then over, except for very infrequent occasions when G-d chose to make supernatural miracles, such as the splitting of the Red Sea.

All creatures that exist today existed from the very beginning. Not a single new creature, nor even a single new organ, has ever come into the world since the time of creation.⁴⁴ This has been our belief since *matan Torah*, and, indeed, even before, in a *mesorah* of testimony that stretches from Adam haRishon through Noach and the *Avos*. Let no one be in a hurry to discard this *mesorah* for any new theories. Theories come and go, but our *emunah* will still remain unchanged.

Let's take a good look at what our *emunah* tells us, and the evidence of our own eyes. This is really our main objective: seeing and realizing the existence of the Creator and His overwhelmingly vast intelligence. Then we'll come back to other theories. Perhaps by then we will have a new perspective on the entire issue.

---

43   This is actually what we celebrate when we keep Shabbos: the conclusion of the supernatural creation of the universe, and the transition to the natural laws of "nature," supervised and maintained by Hashem.

44   Obviously, the prevailing theories disagree with what has been stated here. As far as we are concerned, there is not the slightest evidence to back up their position. More about the lack of evidence will come later.

CHAPTER FOURTEEN

Invisible but Everywhere

Electricity is an invisible energy. No one can see actual electricity itself. Some hundred and fifty years ago, humans learned how to harness this energy to the service of mankind. Today we have various types of machines and technology that are run by electrical power. Although no person has ever seen electricity, no one doubts that there is indeed such an invisible energy.

It is precisely the same with magnetism. Although the magnets are mysteriously drawn together, we do not see the actual magnetism. Nevertheless, we cannot deny its existence.

> שמות פרק לג פסוק כ
> כי לא יראני האדם וחי:
>
> *No man can see Me and live.*

So it is with the Creator, as well. No one can ever see the Creator Himself, but we certainly can "see Him" through His works. Yes! If we open our eyes and our hearts, we **can** see the Creator through the incredible wonders of Nature, which could only have been engineered by an infinite mastermind. In this section, we hope to present a mere sampling of some of these wonders, in order to strengthen our *emunah* in the fundamental belief in a Creator.

WELCOME TO YOUR WORLD

Imagine walking in a desolate place, such as the Sahara desert. As far as you can see in all directions, there is nothing but sand. Nothing would even hint that any other human being ever set foot here before. Suddenly, you come across a pile of ten stones. All the stones are of uniform size, shape and color. They lie in perfect pyramid formation: four on the bottom, three on the next row, two on top of those and one smack in the middle on top. What is the first thought that comes to mind? You wonder, not **how** did the stones get there, but rather **who** put the stones there. The thought that maybe the stones were blown there by a sandstorm, and just happened to land in an orderly fashion, will not even enter your mind. No way! No foolishness of saying "anything is possible," or "given enough time anything can happen," would shake your conviction one iota that these stones were placed here by an intelligent human being who was intent on making a small pyramid. Anyone who would attribute this to some accidental occurrence would be looked on as a fool. Even a simple pyramid of a mere ten stones! All the more so if the base of the pyramid had a thousand stones, rather than just four.

Pyramid-like phenomena, considerably more complex than the thousand-stone-based one we just described, are everywhere. Each one indicates endless plan and purpose. These should inspire us to ask, "Who put this into formation?" Wherever we turn, we find evidence of an infinite intelligence. If we would be paying attention, we would recognize Hashem's signature everywhere. But, obviously, we are so preoccupied with other distractions that we hardly seem to notice.

SEFER CHOVOS HALEVAVOS

There is a classical *sefer* called *Chovos Halevavos*.[45] In it, the author tells us that the very first step to recognizing the Creator is through observing

---

45 Written by Rabbeinu Bachya ibn Paquda over 800 years ago.

His endless wisdom in the natural world around us. This section of the *sefer* is called *Sha'ar Habechinah*. *Bechinah* means delving into nature to see the hand of Hashem. In our time, Rabbi Avigdor Miller *zt"l*, expanded upon this subject in his books and lectures in a most wonderful manner. Many other authors have followed his lead in demonstrating the infinite intelligence in Nature. Much of what will be cited in this section has been taken from those and other sources.[46]

OPEN YOUR EYES TO SEE THE OBVIOUS

The Midrash relates:

> מובא בספר קובץ מאמרים לרבי אלחנן וסרמן זצ"ל (מאמר על האמונה)
> מעשה שבא מין אחד לרבי עקיבא. אמר המין לרבי עקיבא "מי ברא את העולם?" אמר לו רבי עקיבא "הקדוש ברוך הוא". אמר המין "הראני דבר ברור". אמר לו רבי עקיבא "מי ארג את בגדך?" אמר המין "אורג". וכלשון הזה אמר רבי עקיבא לתלמידיו "כשם שהבגד מעיד על האורג והדלת מעידה על הנגר והבית מעיד על הבנאי כך העולם מעיד על הקדוש ברוך הוא שבראו".
>
> *An atheist once challenged Rabbi Akiva, "Who created the world?" Rabbi Akiva answered, "The Holy One, blessed be He." "Show me a clear proof!" demanded the skeptic. Rabbi Akiva said to him, "Who made your garment?" The atheist responded, "A weaver, of course." Rabbi Akiva retorted, "Show me a clear proof!" Now Rabbi Akiva turned to his students and said, "Just as the garment testifies to the existence of the weaver, the door to the carpenter, and the house to the builder, so does the world testify to Hakadosh Baruch Hu Who created it."*

If you are wearing a woolen garment, you know that it didn't look the same as it does now when it was on the back of the sheep. It needed to be shorn, combed, cleaned, dyed, spun into threads, made into cloth, cut to size and sewn together to make a completed article of clothing. All this was done by the garment-maker. Although you may have no idea who he is, you know that there had to be one, because you can't get a jacket without him.

When you sit inside a building, you know there was a builder. The building didn't come about when a tornado ripped through a junk yard

---

[46] Some from Torah sources, others from secular sources.

and picked up scraps of wood, metal, glass, screws and bolts, and just plopped it all down in the shape of a finished building, complete with doors, windows, floors, plumbing and electricity. No! There must have been a builder.

The unbiased human mind cannot accept the possibility that something intricate and complex could result from mere chance. None of us have ever seen complex mechanisms appear randomly from nowhere. All the more so humanity and the world itself. Someone *must* have created all this.

ALL BY ITSELF?

Rabbeinu Bachya, in his above mentioned classic work, *Chovos Halevavos*, tells us how foolish it is to think that something that demonstrates intelligence came about by accident:

> **שער היחוד פרק ו**
>
> ויש בני אדם שאמרו שהעולם נהיה במקרה מבלי בורא ח"ו. ותימה בעיני איך תעלה בדעת מחשבה כזאת? ואילו אמר אדם בגלגל של מים המתגלגל להשקות שדה כי זה נתקן מבלי כוונת אומן היינו חושבים את האומר זה לסכל ומשתגע. ... וידוע כי הדברים אשר הם בלי כוונת מכוין לא ימצאו בהם סימני חכמה. הלא תראה אם ישפך לאדם דיו פתאום על נייר חלק אי אפשר שיצטייר ממנו כתב מסודר. ואילו בא לפנינו כתב מסודר ואחד אמר כי נשפך הדיו על הנייר מעצמו ונעשתה צורת הכתב היינו מכזיבים אותו.

> *There are people who say that the world came into being by accident without a Creator, chas v'shalom. This is a wonder in my eyes. How could someone entertain such a thought? Were a person to say about a water pump that irrigates a field that it was made without any intelligence, that person would be viewed as an absolute insane fool... It is known that things that are made without intelligence behind them will never display signs of wisdom. Don't you see? If someone's ink were to spill out suddenly on a blank piece of paper, it would not be possible that an organized text would be formed from it. If an organized text were to be brought before us, and someone were to say that the ink spilled on to the paper by itself, we would declare him a liar.*

JUST BY ACCIDENT?

Imagine the following scenario: An acquaintance of yours is looking through his wallet in your presence. You notice among his papers a check drawn on your account and signed with your signature. The check is made out to him for five thousand dollars. You know very well that that you never issued such a check. When you confront him, he tells you that an amazing coincidence occurred. He was just going to tell you about it! He found a blank check of yours that had fallen on the floor, and placed it on the table next to an open bottle of ink. The bottle tipped over and the ink spilled out. Sheerly by accident, it just happened to form the writing on the check; signature, amount payable, and name of payee. Even if your friend had a reputation for scrupulous honesty, there is no way you would believe something so preposterous. Such a claim would be laughed out of a court of law. An ink spill will never form a cohesive sentence!

The wonders of the universe are so numerous and so complex, that to explain them away without recognizing the intelligence behind them is more ludicrous than saying that the Encyclopedia Britannica was written by the spillage of a tanker full of ink into a paper factory!

Although we are not yet ready to deal with the theory of the Big Bang or the theory of evolution right now, let it suffice to reiterate that these popularly accepted theories would have us believe that there is no intelligence behind any of the natural phenomena in the universe. They are saying that everything came about through a series of lucky chances.[47] But your own eyes and your mind tell you clearly that this cannot be.

If a spilled inkwell could never write out a coherent sentence, could any sensible person attribute the trillions of intricacies in nature to mere chance? Could the human body with its countless complex systems have come about haphazardly? Each and every member of the plant, animal and insect kingdoms possesses the mechanisms and instincts that it needs to survive and reproduce. No two species are alike. The perfect order of the heavenly bodies, and the perfect balance in the natural world (when

---

[47] The evolutionists will tell you that it is not so, but we will yet see that according to their theory, it all amounts to nothing more than happy accidents.

untampered with by man), cannot be assigned to mere luck or chance. The signature of the Creator is clearly imprinted wherever we turn.

THE INCREDIBLE REPLICA

An enlightening story is told about the famous scientist Isaac Newton,[48] who was a very strong believer in G-d. He was visited by another scientist, who was an atheist. The atheist asked him how such an educated man could believe in G-d. Newton became very serious, and told him that he wants to show him something of great interest. He took him into his workshop and removed from a shelf a model of the solar system made of balls, wheels and springs. He told him, "This is a model of the nine planets in our solar system. Here is Earth, with the moon around it, here is Jupiter and its numerous moons, here is Venus, etc." He pulled on a string and all the components began to revolve in their exact orbit, just as they do in the heavens. The guest was amazed, and said, "Newton, how did you make this?" Newton answered him with feigned calmness. "I? I didn't make it at all. A pile of balls, wheels and springs was lying in my courtyard. A dog was chasing a cat and they ran straight into the pile. Everything started flying around. I heard the commotion, and came out of my house to discover that when it all landed, everything just happened to fall into this formation." The astonished guest said that it is incredible that such a coordinated model could be made by itself. Whereupon Newton responded, "This model is but a poor replica of the actual heavens. If it is clear to you that the model could not come into being by accident, how then can you possibly think that the vast original came into existence without a Creator?"

There is nothing haphazard in outer space. Every heavenly body follows a prescribed orbit to perfection. Indeed, the *navi* Yeshaya tells us to look up at the sky and realize who made all this.

ישעיה פרק מא פסוק כו

שאו מרום עיניכם וראו מי ברא אלה המוציא במספר צבאם לכלם בשם יקרא מרב אונים ואמיץ כח איש לא נעדר:

---

48 Rav Yosef Gabai, *Mesilos el HaEmunah* 1998, vol. 1, p. 20.

> Lift up your eyes on high and see: Who created these? (It is) He Who brings forth their host by number. He calls each one by name. (This is) from the one Who is Almighty and great of strength. He doesn't miss even one.

Dovid haMelech tells us a similar message in *Tehillim*:

> תהלים פרק יט פסוק ב
>
> השמים מספרים כבוד ק-ל ומעשה ידיו מגיד הרקיע
>
> The heavens declare the glory of Hashem, and the sky tells the work of His Hands.

The author of *Chovos Halevavos* tells us that the most effective way to recognize the Creator is by studying the marvels of the natural world.

> חובות הלבבות בהקדמה לשער השני
>
> והיתה הבחינה בחכמה הנראית בבריאות הבורא יתעלה הדרך הקרובה ביותר אל ברור מציאותו והנתיב הסלול לדעת אמיתתו
>
> Discerning the wisdom which can be seen in the creations of the Creator, may He be exalted, is the closest (most effective) way to clarifying His existence, and the trodden path to knowing the truth about Him.

The Rambam, as well, tells us that studying the wisdom of Hashem in the world is the way to come to love and fear Him.

> רמב״ם הלכות יסודי התורה פרק ב הלכה ב
>
> והיאך היא הדרך לאהבתו ויראתו, בשעה שיתבונן האדם במעשיו וברואיו הנפלאים הגדולים ויראה מהן חכמתו שאין לה ערך ולא קץ מיד הוא אוהב ומשבח ומפאר ומתאוה תאוה גדולה לידע השם הגדול כמו שאמר דוד צמאה נפשי לאלקים לק-ל חי. וכשמחשב בדברים האלו עצמן מיד הוא נרתע לאחוריו ויפחד ויודע שהוא בריה קטנה שפלה אפלה עומדת בדעת קלה מעוטה לפני תמים דעות כמו שאמר דוד כי אראה שמיך מעשה אצבעותיך מה אנוש כי תזכרנו
>
> What is the way to come to love Him and fear Him? When a person thinks about His marvelous great deeds and creations, he will see that His wisdom has no end and cannot be measured. Immediately he will love, praise, glorify and long with a great longing to know His great name. As Dovid haMelech

> said, "My soul thirsts for Elokim, the living G-d." When he thinks about these things, he will immediately be taken aback, awestricken, and know that he is a very small and humble creature, who stands with a small limited mind before the Supreme Intelligence. As Dovid haMelech said, "When I see Your heavens, the work of Your fingers, (I say), 'What is a person that You should consider him?'"

AN OLD SYSTEM

The idea of discovering the Creator by observing His universe is nothing new. Our father Avraham did exactly that, long ago. This is what the Rambam tells us:

> **רמב"ם הלכות עבודה זרה פרק א הלכה ג**
>
> כיון שנגמל איתן זה התחיל לשוטט בדעתו והוא קטן והתחיל לחשוב ביום ובלילה והיה תמיה היאך אפשר שיהיה הגלגל הזה נוהג תמיד ולא יהיה לו מנהיג ומי יסבב אותו, כי אי אפשר שיסבב את עצמו, ולא היה לו מלמד ולא מודיע דבר אלא מושקע באור כשדים בין עובדי כוכבים הטפשים ואביו ואמו וכל העם עובדי כוכבים והוא עובד עמהם ולבו משוטט ומבין עד שהשיג דרך האמת והבין קו הצדק מתבונתו הנכונה, וידע שיש שם אלוה אחד והוא מנהיג הגלגל והוא ברא הכל ואין בכל הנמצא אלוה חוץ ממנו, וידע שכל העולם טועים ודבר שגרם להם לטעות זה שעובדים את הכוכבים ואת הצורות עד שאבד האמת מדעתם. ובן ארבעים שנה הכיר אברהם את בוראו
>
> *From the time this giant intellect was weaned, his mind began to search, even while he was still a child. He began to think by day and by night, wondering, how could it be possible that this universe should function constantly without anyone controlling it and making it go around. It certainly cannot make itself go around. He had no teacher, nor anyone to inform him of anything. Rather, he was immersed in Ur Kasdim between the foolish idol worshippers. His father and mother and all the people worshipped idols, and he worshipped with them. [But while he was worshipping,] his heart was soaring to understand, until he arrived at the way of truth and understood the line of righteousness from his upright intelligence. He knew that there is only one G-d. It is He who controls the universe and He Who created everything. In all that exists, there is no other G-d besides Him. He knew that the whole world was in error, and it was the worship of the stars which caused them to make*

> *this error, until the truth was lost from their minds. Avraham was forty years old when he recognized his Creator. (He began at age three and came to the full emunah at age forty.)*

IN AVRAHAM AVINU'S FOOTSTEPS

Although we may not possess the genius of our first forefather, whose original thinking led him to discover his Creator, we certainly can follow in his footsteps. If we open our eyes and let our minds soar, as his did, we will surely arrive at the same conclusion as Avraham Avinu.

CHAPTER FIFTEEN

Plan and Purpose

Wherever we look, we see endless plan and purpose. Because we are accustomed to seeing all this since our infancy, we have become so desensitized that we really don't take notice of the wonders around us. However, when we finally stop and take a good look, we will be overwhelmed by the infinite wisdom in the world.

A SUPERFICIAL GLANCE

Even a superficial glance will indicate beyond a doubt that the world has been designed by a highly intelligent being. Whatever denotes intelligence had to be put there by an intelligent being. When we look at the incredible intelligence behind every plant and animal, every organ and limb, and even in the inorganic world, we will stand back in total awe of Hakadosh Baruch Hu. Even before peeking into nature at the molecular level, which can stagger the mind, we will already be overwhelmed by just a surface review of the everyday things we have come to take for granted. Remember that the theorists want to tell us that there is no intelligence involved here at all. In a chaotic world, we should find chaos everywhere, but we actually find only organized complexity wherever we look, cunning design at every turn. This study is endless, and we could spend our entire lives thinking about this, without even having scratched the surface. But that won't discourage us from at least getting started. So here we go.

FINE-TUNED FOR LIFE

In order to have life on Earth, many things must be "just so." The conditions needed to support life on Earth are so numerous that we cannot possibly list them here, but we certainly can't pass up the opportunity to mention a few. Scientists now know that there are trillions of stars in space. Each one is a different size and has a different surface temperature. Of all these trillions of stars, only our sun is perfectly suited for us. If it were even slightly bigger or hotter, everything on Earth would be burned to a crisp. The same would happen if the sun were any closer to Earth. On the other hand, if the sun were any smaller or further away from Earth, everything on our planet would freeze.

Gravity is a force that pulls things together. If not for gravity, the planets would not stay in their orbits. The strength of gravity is not the same all over the universe. On Mars, the gravity is sixty percent less than on Earth. On the moon, it is only a fraction of what it is on Earth. With less gravity, we would float away. If, on the other hand, the force of gravity on Earth were stronger, we would smash into the ground. Our planet's gravity is just perfectly fine-tuned for life on Earth.

The atmosphere is the layer of air that surrounds Earth. "The atmosphere is an important part of what makes Earth livable. It blocks some of the sun's dangerous rays from reaching Earth. It traps heat, making Earth a comfortable temperature. And the oxygen within our atmosphere is essential for life."[49] All living beings on Earth need oxygen. However, pure oxygen would be harmful. Our atmosphere has just the right blend of (mostly) nitrogen, twenty-one percent oxygen, plus one percent of some other gasses. The proportion is perfect for our needs.

All life on Earth depends on water. Humans, animals and all vegetation are composed mostly of water. Other planets do not have water. Only

---

49   http://www.windows2universe.org/earth/Atmosphere/overview.html

Earth has water. Water acts in a very mysterious way. All other things become denser (heavier) as they become colder. Water is the only exception to this rule. When it reaches a temperature of four degrees Celsius, it becomes lighter rather than heavier. That is the reason why ice cubes float in a cup of soda — because they are lighter than the water they displace. If not for this, life on Earth could not exist. The lakes and rivers would all freeze over in winter, and the first layer of ice would sink to the bottom. Then another layer would freeze over, and this process would repeat itself until the entire lake or river would become a solid block of ice. All the marine life would perish and the underwater plants would die. The waterways would become polluted, and the water would be undrinkable. Animals whose main food is fish would die of hunger. So, it just works out (luckily?) that water doesn't follow the same rule that everything else on Earth does.[50]

CYCLES AND RECYCLING

Ever walk through a forest of very tall trees? Every autumn, all their leaves drop off onto the forest floor. Many of those trees may be hundreds of years old. You would expect to wade through hundreds of years of leaves to get through the forest, but you don't have to at all. Where did all those leaves go? Bacteria in the soil decompose the leaves, and they in turn replenish the soil with nutrients. This is a pattern throughout the natural world, that things are recycled, over and over again. Even the dead bodies of animals (and humans) eventually decay and return to the soil. As a result, our vital resources do not get used up.

As mentioned, all animals, as well as humans, need oxygen. Our atmosphere contains oxygen, among other gasses. We inhale oxygen with

---

50 In a recent Wall Street Journal article (Dec. '14) entitled, "Science Increasingly Makes the Case for G-d," it states that scientists have begun retreating from their former position. They used to think that only two conditions are needed for a planet to support life: the right kind of star and a planet the right distance from that star. Hence they thought that there could be life on any of 1,000,000,000,000,000,000,000,000 planets. Now they know that there are at least two hundred conditions necessary to support life, and that it is astounding that planet Earth just happens to meet them all. Theoretical physicist Paul Davies is quoted as saying, "The appearance of design is overwhelming."

every breath we take. If you are in a room full of people and there are no windows open, the room begins to get stuffy. That is because the crowd has already used up some of the oxygen in the room. Why doesn't the oxygen supply on the earth get used up? The answer is that when we breathe in oxygen, we exhale carbon dioxide. Plants take in the carbon dioxide and give off oxygen. A perfect balance. There are vast forests surrounding the Arctic Circle. An unthinking person might assume that they serve no purpose. The truth, however, is that they produce about a quarter of the world's supply of oxygen. (If we will just open our eyes we will see that everything in the universe serves a designated purpose.)

The sun pumps up vast amounts of water into the atmosphere by evaporation, forming clouds. The water in the clouds would be useless if not for the wind. The wind blows the clouds over the continents, and the rain falls to the earth through the power of gravity. The rain irrigates the soil, runs into underground streams, and eventually flows back to the ocean. The process is started anew. This is the pattern of recycling, which is evident throughout everything in all of nature. All of creation is full of this magnificent wisdom and planning.

CHAPTER SIXTEEN

Tools and Accessories

*I*magine that we see three toolboxes lying on the table in front of us. One has only plumber's tools, the second contains electrician's tools and the third a full set of carpenter's tools. Only a fool would say that these tool boxes were filled by someone randomly dumping tools into each box. No! Surely the tools were placed inside with a plan. There was an intention that each box should have the tools needed for one of these craftsmen.

If we observe the myriad creatures in our world, we will see precisely the same thing. Every creature on earth has been provided with the exact set of tools and accessories that it needs for its particular mode of life and survival. The Creator has given each one the organs, instincts and the tools needed to live, find food, build a nest or den, reproduce, escape predators and survive the winter. Not only do they have everything they need, but they have no extra, unneeded organs or instincts. No two are exactly alike, each one possessing its unique full set of tools to be what it is, and exist and survive as it does. (If once in a while we find an organ whose use we do not know, we need only be patient and eventually we will discover its purpose.) It is blatantly obvious that each one was designed to be exactly what it is. A few examples can start us on a lifetime career of seeing the wisdom of the *Borei Olam* in action. Each one has many more tools than described here, each one perfectly designed for the successful functioning of that creature. The examples are endless, but this book is not, so we can only give a little taste.

INSTINCTS

Every creature on earth has been endowed with the instincts that it needs for its existence. An instinct means that the creature has the knowledge of what it needs to do without being taught. No one has any idea how each creature came to have that particular skill, but somehow it does. The baby duckling can swim as soon as it reaches water, without swimming lessons, even when its mother is not present. The spider knows how to spin a web to catch its prey. A newborn baby (of any species) knows to suckle from its mother. The newborn kangaroo knows how to find its mother's pouch immediately after birth. Salmon know how to find their place of birth, to which they swim upstream to spawn. The caribou don't need a map to know how to migrate two thousand miles to find food when the seasons change. Birds that migrate can fly thousands of miles and find the exact spot where they need to spend the winter. They also know how to fly in a special formation, which enables them to use the wind to their advantage. A newborn calf doesn't need to be taught to eat grass. It just knows. The robin knows how to build a nest. The bee knows how to make a hive. The bear can tell when it's time to find a den in which to hibernate through the winter. The list goes on and on. How did they get this knowledge? By chance? By accident? Every single species on earth?

PLANTS

Trees

Every leaf needs its space in the sun. The branches of trees never grow directly one on top of the other, but are so spaced that the leaves on every branch will get their share of the sunlight. As well, no two leaves grow right on top of each other, on any tree in the world. They, too, are positioned so that each one will get a portion of the sun's rays.

How do the water and the nutrients go against the force of gravity and reach even the highest parts of the tree? Scientists have a theory that they call the cohesion-tension theory. It's quite complicated, and, after all is said and done, it's only a theory. The tree knows nothing about the theory, but is nevertheless able to transport all the nutrients upwards. It was simply designed to do so.

Take an apple seed and plant it in a very large tub of earth, after measuring the amount of earth. Leave it in a sunny place and keep watering it until eventually it grows into an apple tree. Carefully remove the apple tree and measure the amount of earth in the tub. It will be approximately the same amount you started with. From where do the materials in the apple tree come? Obviously not from earth "transformed" into wood, since the earth is still there! The wood and other materials are a product of nothing but water, sunlight and some nutrients from the soil. Ingenious!

Seeds

A seed that has fallen to the ground will always send the roots downward into the soil and the stem up from the ground, regardless of what position it landed in. Every seed has a system by which it gets planted. Some are carried by the wind, while others attach themselves to animals by way of burrs that catch on to whatever passes by. The peach seed is encased in a pit that is harder than any other wood in the tree. It cannot be sawed through. It has a seam of glue around it, which will not dissolve even in very hot water. But when the pit falls to the ground, microbes in the soil eat through the glue in the seam, and the seed inside germinates. Every seed contains DNA, the blueprint for the entire plant. Plan and purpose!

Fruits

All fruits are drab when unripe, and get their beautiful coloring only when ripe for eating. Coloring is found only on the outside, where it is needed to attract the eater. Never is the inside of a peel colored. The outer peel of the fruit is waterproof, enabling the fruit to last long periods of time even after picking. The juice inside the fruits does not run off when the fruit is cut. Rather, it is cunningly combined with the meat of the fruit. Unripe fruits are very hard to pluck off the tree. After the fruit is ready, an inner-timing mechanism causes the stem to release its hold and the fruit is easily picked. Should the fruit stay on too long, however, the tree will release it completely and the fruit will drop to the ground. The fruits were designed for eating.

Bananas

Ever notice the strings inside the banana peel? They seem to serve no purpose. Indeed, in a world that supposedly evolved by chance, there ought to be many things that have no purposeful function. Since this world was created by a Master Intelligence, we know that there is nothing in the natural world without purpose. The strings are called phloem bundles. They are part of the system that carries nutrition to all parts of the banana. Nothing is random. Everything is designed for a purpose.

INSECTS

Mosquito

This insect is not popular: the mosquito. Some types of mosquitoes live on blood that they take out of animals and people. Only the female sucks blood, because she needs the high level of protein in order to produce her eggs. She has the digestive system to turn the blood into these nutrients. Other creatures could not exist if they had nothing but blood to eat. They don't have the machinery to process it. The mosquito does have that equipment, and many more accessories. The mouthparts of the females are perfectly shaped like a hypodermic needle for piercing the skin of animal hosts. Just before drawing the blood, the mosquito injects saliva into the body of the host. This saliva contains an anticoagulant; without it, the female mosquito's proboscis (needle-like mouth) would become clogged with blood clots. Quite some tool!

Before the mosquito bites, she applies a topical anesthetic which prevents the person being bitten from feeling the bite just long enough for the mosquito to fly safely away before you swat it. Mosquito tools!

Butterfly

The author of *Tiferes Yisrael*, a commentary on the Mishnah, tells us the following amazing point: One of the thirteen principles of our faith is the belief in the resurrection of the dead, *techiyas ha-meisim*. If you want to see a perfect example of this, all we have to do is look at the butterfly. It starts off life as a caterpillar, and weaves a cocoon around itself. Inside the cocoon, the caterpillar disintegrates to a liquid mush. Somehow, processes we do not understand begin to take place. In the end, a beautiful live butterfly emerges, with all the body parts and functions needed for a butterfly. An accident?

The Monarch butterfly migrates from central Mexico to the northeastern United States or southern Canada. The butterflies that left Mexico lay eggs along the way and die, since they have a lifespan of only one month, too short to finish the trip. Their offspring continue the trip. This process is repeated a few times. The last group, however, has a life span of nine months, and returns back to the original home, often to the exact same tree that its ancestors started from.

Honeybee

The bee has every tool that it needs for its existence and survival, as well as for its most vital function of pollinating fruit trees. Without the bee to pollinate the trees, we would have no apples, cherries, and many other fruits and flowers. So the bee has brushes on its legs with which to brush the pollen into baskets on its body. It lives off the nectar that it finds inside the flowers. Without the nectar in the flowers, the bees would have no food source. Nectar evaporates rapidly, so inside its body, the bee has a factory that produces an enzyme which turns nectar into honey. (Honey does not evaporate.) Another factory produces wax, with which the bee knows instinctively to build a hive with perfectly shaped hexagonal cells to store the honey. The queen bee also lays her eggs in these cubicles. Honeybees have a very distinct social order, with each type of bee performing only its designated functions. Bee tools!

SEA CREATURES

Fish

It's not a small feat to be able to breathe underwater. You need special equipment to accomplish this. Fish are equipped with all the necessary equipment. Oxygen dissolved in the water passes through thin gill membranes into the fish's blood, and is then pumped around the body.

Octopus

The octopus would make a good meal for some predators. When pursued, it gives off a screen of black ink that hides it from the predator's sight while it escapes. Special skin cells called chromatophores enable octopi to blend into their background and hide. They can instantaneously make themselves look like a rock (or anything else) in order to sneak up on their prey. They can hide in very narrow crevices; because their body is so soft it can squeeze in. If an octopus needs to get away in a hurry, it uses jet propulsion by contracting their mantle and expelling a jet of water that propels them forward. A full set of octopus accessories!

Blue Whale

The blue whale is perfectly streamlined to be able to move at maximum speed. Although it is the largest creature on earth, it lives on tiny shrimp-like creatures called krill. These are found in the ocean in millions. Krill are not found everywhere at all times. The blue whale migrates thousands of kilometers from its summer-breeding grounds to its winter-feeding grounds. It needs no GPS to guide it, for it knows the way precisely, and knows just when to find the krill. How does this giant creature trap these tiny krill? It has no teeth. Instead it has an upper and lower jaw made out of whale bone, called baleen. It is like a sifter full of holes, made out of bone. The whale opens up its monstrous jaws, sucks in very large amounts of water, and then squirts out the water through the holes in the baleen. The krill don't fit through the holes, so he gets his meal this way. Made to order for the blue whale!

The Weddell (Antarctic) Seal

There is a certain type of seal that lives in Antarctica, called the Weddell seal. It is much too cold for this seal to survive the winter on land. The water is much warmer, so the seal stays in the water all winter long. It fishes under water for its food. However, the seal needs to come up for air every few minutes, and all the waterways freeze solid during the winter.

How does he breathe? This seal has teeth that are shaped like ice picks. As soon as the water starts to freeze over, each time it needs to take a breath it comes up and chops the ice around its air hole, in order to keep it open all winter. Other creatures cannot chop ice with their teeth, only this one, whose survival depends on it.

LAND MAMMALS

Mammals are among the most complex beings on earth. Each one has been provided with everything it needs to live its distinct mode of life. The examples could go on and on, so we present merely a few.

Star-nosed mole

This mole is one of the oddest-looking creatures on the planet. It lives underground and feeds on worms or other small creatures. It is basically blind, so how does it find its food? It has twenty-two tentacles (feelers) around its nose. Each one has thousands of sensory receptors, so it makes up for lack of sight with its heightened sense of touch. Although it cannot see, when it presses these tentacles against the ground, they transmit a three-dimensional picture of the terrain to its brain, the equivalent of a mental sonogram.

Grizzly bear

The grizzly bear's main hunting tool is his exceptional sense of smell, one of the most powerful on earth. The scent detecting area of a grizzly's nose is one hundred times larger than that of a human nose. It bristles with over a billion receptor cells, connected to over ten million nerve cells. This enables the grizzly to detect the scent of another bear, garbage (which they eat), or a carcass from over a mile away. The ability to smell is what keeps the grizzly bear alive.

Cat

Cats catch and eat mice, by sneaking up and pouncing on them with their claws. These claws are retractable, so that the cat's soft paws make no sound, allowing it to surprise its prey. They have a sensory organ at the end of their whiskers called a proprioceptor, which sends tactile signals to the brain and nervous system. Whiskers help the cat gauge whether it can fit into a tight space (without even being able to see it). Whiskers do much more, however. They enable the cat to respond to vibrations in the air, such as when the cat is chasing prey, and to visually measure distance, which is why they are able to leap so quickly and gracefully onto a narrow ledge or out of harm's way. Designed to catch mice!

Beaver

The beaver needs to build a dam so that the pond or lake he lives in will be deep enough to store his supply of food in it. For this purpose, he has front teeth that are as sharp as an axe. With these teeth he is able to chop down trees. He uses them constantly, and they wear down. An ax needs to be resharpened regularly, but the beaver's teeth rejuvenate and grow back sharpened again. Otherwise, the beaver could not survive. He has the instinct to chop down the tree at just the right angle, so that it falls exactly where he wants it. Since he spends a lot of time underwater, he has hind legs like oars that propel him through the water, a tail shaped like a rudder, and transparent membranes that cover his eyes, so he can remain under water for a long time with full vision. Beaver tools!

BIRDS

Bones and feathers

Birds' bones are hollow, very different than the solid bones of other creatures. If birds' bones were also solid, the birds would be too heavy to fly. But hollow bones would break easily, so they have well-spaced cross-braces to strengthen them.[51]

All birds have feathers, but each one has the type of feathers it needs for existence. The eagle has very different feathers than the American dipper, each custom tailored to its needs. Each bird has various types of feathers, each serving different purposes. Contour feathers provide the bird with color and give the bird its shape. The largest of these are wing feathers,

---

51 The encyclopedia words it this way: "The bird skeleton is highly adapted for flight. Birds have many bones that are hollow (pneumatized) with criss-crossing struts or trusses for structural strength." Adapted? Nothing random here – incredible design.

strong and stiff, supporting the bird during flight. Tail feathers are used to provide stability and control. Feathers on both the upper and lower sides of the body help streamline the shape of the wings and tail, while providing the bird with insulation. Down feathers are made in such a way that they create a puffy tangle of insulating air pockets, to keep the bird warm. There are still more types, but the point is clear. Each is designed to fulfill a specific function, and the plan and purpose with which they were created is too obvious for an honest person to ignore.

Eggshells

All birds lay eggs, but the thickness of the eggshell varies from species to species. If the shell were too thick for a small type of bird, the chick would not be able to peck its way out. On the other hand, if the shell were too thin for a larger kind of bird, it would crack under the pressure of being laid by the mother bird. Therefore, every single species of bird on earth produces eggs that are tailor-made to be just the right thickness for that kind of bird: not too thick and not too thin. Some birds,[52] whose beak is not sharp enough to break through the shell, have a temporary hook called an eyetooth on their beak. With this hook, the chick makes the first hole in the shell, and is then able to peck its way out. Then the eyetooth falls off. Quite a tool!

Woodpecker

The woodpecker has an entire set of woodpecker tools. With his chisel-shaped beak, he drills holes in the bark of trees to get the bugs that live under the bark. His tongue is exceptionally long and has bristles on it to be able to reach and grab for the bugs. He knows instinctively how to drill in perfect straight lines, vertically and horizontally. That way he doesn't miss out on any spots where his food hides. The flying sawdust does not harm his eyes, because two membranes come down over his eyes automatically, just prior to pecking. He can remain suspended on the tree effortlessly because he has four claws to get a full grip on the tree, the outer two facing frontward, the inner two facing backward. He also has a

---

52 Such as the chicken.

long, stiff tail that he locks into place like a brace to hold him comfortably up. He doesn't get a concussion while banging his head against a tree or pole dozens of times per minute. The bones between the beak and skull are not rigidly joined. Instead, the connective tissue is spongy and elastic, serving as a shock absorber. Woodpecker tools!

Emperor Penguin

This penguin lives in Antarctica, the coldest place on earth. In order for the newborn chicks to fledge (become self-sufficient) in time for the summer, their eggs must be laid just during the cold of winter. The chick would freeze inside the egg, but the male penguin has a flap of thick fur between its legs and places the egg there all winter long. No other bird has this flap of fur, because no other bird needs it. They have a specially engineered counter-current circulatory system that provides an efficient mechanism for retaining heat within the body. Their scale-like feathers are tightly packed in multiple layers that only the harshest winds can ruffle. The feet are strongly clawed for gripping the ice. Emperor penguin tools, perfectly designed!

REPTILES

Alligator

All over the jaws of alligators (and all related creatures, such as crocodiles), there are pimple-like bumps. Scientists discovered that, "these bumps are connected to a nerve called a trigeminal nerve which stimulates the skin and muscles of the face. These nerves travel through holes in the bones of the jaw called foramina that take the nerves to the brain. They are sensors that detect any change that happens in the water of the pond where the animal lives. When you put your finger into the water, the ripples that are sent out make the nerves in the bumps on the alligator's jaws fire, and the animal comes to see what caused the ripples." That's how the alligator finds his prey. Nothing in the universe is purposeless.

The top of the alligator's hide is comprised of square bumps, seemingly only for design, perfect for making alligator skin accessories. But nothing in Hashem's world is without purpose, and those bumps serve a vital purpose for the alligator. All reptiles are cold-blooded. Unlike mammals, whose body produces its own heat (warm-blooded), reptiles (which are cold-blooded) take on the temperature of their surroundings. The raised scales, called scutes, on an alligator's back contain deposits of calcium called osteoderms. If an alligator gets too cold, it needs to bask in the sun. The osteoderms in an alligator's back increase the animal's blood flow to the area, and help to rapidly transmit heat from its back into the rest of its body.

The muscles which open the jaws of the alligator are very weak. They have only twenty pounds of pressure per square inch. However, when the alligator pounces on its prey by surprise, it needs to come down very quickly and with force, so as to surprise its victim and hold it tight from getting away. Therefore, the muscles that close the alligator's jaws have one thousand pounds of pressure per square inch. The alligator has a special valve at the back of his throat that allows him to open his mouth and eat food underwater without choking. Alligator tools!

CHAPTER SEVENTEEN

Humans

*I*f we were to spend the rest of our lives doing nothing else but describing the wonders of the human body, we would never run out of material to speak about. We will start only with superficial, surface wonders. Then we'll give a few examples of the more complex inner workings of the systems operating in our bodies.

ENJOY THAT APPLE

The miracle of eating and digesting something as simple as an apple should not be taken for granted. Before we start, we must know that the body cannot use an apple in its present form. It needs to break it down, extract from it the parts the body can use, and then discard the rest. Countless mechanisms and chemical factories are employed in this process. In order to get any benefit whatsoever from that apple, many systems have to be put to work.

Once you've decided that you'd like to eat an apple, your body is already at work. You begin to salivate in anticipation of your snack. The saliva in your mouth is excreted by the salivary glands and is composed of chemicals that begin the digestive process by breaking down starches into smaller molecules.

The front teeth are designed to enable you to bite off a piece, and the tongue moves it to the back teeth, where it will be chewed into a consistency that the body can digest. (Imagine how difficult it would be to eat an apple if the grinding teeth would be in front and the biting teeth would be in back.) The tongue gets busy sorting out any part of the apple that you don't desire to eat, such as the seeds or part of the core.

A flap called the epiglottis moves automatically into place to cover your windpipe so that none of the apple will go down the wrong pipe and cause you to choke. Into the esophagus (food pipe) goes the apple. The esophagus is a long tube that runs from the mouth to the stomach. The food will go down, even if the eater is lying upside down, because the esophagus uses rhythmic, wave-like muscle movements, called peristalsis, to force food from the throat into the stomach.

At the bottom of the food pipe, there is a one-way valve that only allows food to enter, but prevents the acid in the stomach from backing up the food pipe and damaging it. People in whom this valve is malfunctioning have a painful condition called acid reflux.

In the top of your stomach are one million glands that secrete acid to burn up the food and transform it into something usable by the body. Acid burns terribly, but your stomach is not harmed, because there is a special stomach lining which is impervious to the acid. (No such lining exists anywhere else in the body, only in the stomach where it is needed.)

The acid (together with enzymes secreted by the cells of the stomach) break down protein into smaller fragments containing amino acids, fats into fatty acids, and starch and sugars into simple sugars. For example, the sugar that is found on our tables is sucrose, which is made up of two simple sugars, fructose and glucose. Glucose is needed to nourish the brain, which cannot use any other nutrient. The food is turned into a thick liquid called chyme.

The chyme is pushed by contraction of the stomach muscles into the first part of the small intestine called the duodenum. The presence of chyme in the duodenum causes the pancreas to secrete chemicals to neutralize the stomach acids, and enzymes to break down the food some more. At this point, the proteins have been broken down into amino acids, the fats into small chain fatty acids and the starches into simple sugars.

Fat and fatty acids do not mix with water. (Think of chicken soup with the fat globules floating on top of the soup.) The content of the small intestine is mainly water. In order to digest the fatty acids, the liver, through the common bile duct, secretes bile into the duodenum. Bile is a chemical with two ends. The one end sticks to fats and the other to water. This allows the fatty acids to travel as very small amounts of fat within the material in the small intestine. The different nutrients are absorbed into the blood stream in the small intestine. There are millions of finger-like projections coating the wall of the small intestines called villi. The villi contain blood vessels in their inner part. The cells on the outside of the villi grab hold of the different nutrients and actively transport them inside the villus to the blood vessels.

In general, blood vessels either travel away from the heart (arteries) or toward the heart (veins). Arteries have thick walls containing elastic fiber and veins have thin walls. In the digestive system, there is a special arrangement of veins draining the small intestine, which flow directly to the liver, called the portal veins. These veins carry the sugars, fatty acids and amino acids straight to the liver. The liver takes these nutrients and uses them to build protein, fats and starches that are compatible with our bodies. The newly built chemicals exit through the hepatic veins back to the heart, where they are sent where needed.

The digestive system requires a very active blood flow to work, and a greater percentage of blood pumped by the heart is diverted to the stomach and intestines during digestion. Digestion requires coordination of the stomach and different parts of the small intestine. This coordination is achieved by the vagus nerve. This nerve starts in the brainstem, the last part of the brain before the spinal cord. The branches of this nerve are found all over the stomach, small intestine and large intestine. The contraction of the muscles of the stomach and small intestine is directly controlled by the vagus nerve, and coordinated by that nerve, without requiring any thought on the part of the eater.

Think about all the systems and factories that are employed in digesting that apple. How could this intricate coordination be the result of thousands, or even millions, of random mutations, unguided by any intelligence?

VOCAL CORDS

Your ability to talk is thanks to your vocal cords. They produce sound when the air you breathe strikes the cord. That's why the vocal cords are located in your throat right in the path of the incoming breath.

BODY HEAT AND VENTILATION

Your body produces heat, just as any machine does. Somewhere on the back of your refrigerator or your computer there is a vent that lets out the hot air. Your body is no different. For this purpose, you have four million pores on your skin, which let out heat in the form of sweat.

THE HUMAN FACE

Everything on your face protrudes. Your nose, your lips and your ears all stick out. Only the eyes are recessed. If the eyes would protrude like the nose does, any blow might harm the very fragile, intricate machinery. Instead, if something hits you on the face, the bony ridge around the eyes absorbs most of the impact. The eyebrows prevent sweat from running straight into your eyes, and blinking your eyelids and your eyelashes (which is done automatically) keeps out dust and insects.

THE BLOODSTREAM AND THE LIVER

There are sixty trillion cells in your body. Each one needs oxygen constantly, as well as a regular supply of nutrients. Not all cells have the same diet. Calcium in your brain would be deadly. How do all the supplies get delivered to the cells? The bloodstream is the delivery service. It supplies all the cells in your body with everything they need. For this reason, there are blood vessels located everywhere in your body — in order to service all sixty trillion cells. If all your blood vessels were to be stretched out in a straight line, it would stretch for 96,000 miles (enough to go around the earth four times)! All in your one little body.

The blood in your body does not stand still. It is constantly circulating because of the great pump — the heart — that keeps it moving. It would seem that if the blood is circulating under pressure, every time you get a cut it should all just keep on squirting out. No problem. There is a coagulant in the blood that makes it clot and block up the exit. That's why you get a scab over the cut. Why doesn't that same coagulant cause the blood to stop flowing while inside your body? This, too, is no problem. The coagulant only does its work when it hits the oxygen in the air. Inside the body, it does not clot the blood. Accident or perfect design?

The liver, which weighs only about three pounds, performs over five hundred functions in your body.

THE LUNGS

In order for you to get a sufficient oxygen supply, very large amounts of oxygen must be absorbed into the blood stream constantly. How does this happen? When you take a breath, the air goes down the windpipe, into the trachea, into the bronchi and then enters the lungs. In the lungs are air sacs called alveoli. If viewed from the outside, these would look like little clusters of grapes. They consist of many round grape-like shaped balls, each lined with blood vessels. This enables the body to have the largest possible surface to get the oxygen into the bloodstream. How many alveoli are there in your lungs? Only a mere seven hundred million! Although logic would dictate that the air sacs should collapse when we exhale, they do not, because each one has a special tiny cell in it that produces a chemical which prevents the cell from collapsing when the air is emptied out. These very same air sacs help us rid the body of carbon dioxide. When you breathe out, the body delivers carbon dioxide to the alveoli, and you release it in your exhalation.

CHILDBIRTH

The miracles of childbirth are truly astounding. The baby is formed inside the mother's womb and receives nutrition from the mother's blood via the umbilical cord. The fetus is in a sac of water, which absorbs the shocks of the mother's movements. When the baby is fully formed, the passageway expands for the baby to exit the womb. After birth, this passageway returns to normal size.

Only a woman who gives birth produces milk. The first four days, the baby has enough nutrition left in its body from what it took in before birth. No milk is yet needed. However, the baby is susceptible to disease and also needs its system flushed. So, the first four days the mother produces a different liquid, called colostrum, which is full of antibodies and flushes out the system. When the baby needs milk, the mother's body begins producing it!

While inside the mother, the baby gets its oxygen from the mother's bloodstream. The baby's lungs are not needed. In the baby's heart, there is a special tube[53] that goes from one side of the heart to the other, circumventing the lungs. Precisely at the moment of birth, however, the baby needs to breathe oxygen through its lungs. Exactly at that moment, the tube closes up (forever), and the blood begins to circulate through the baby's lungs in time for it to take its first breath.

When the embryo is being formed, the brain sends out fifty thousand nerve endings towards the partially formed eyes. The eyes, in turn, send out fifty thousand nerve endings towards the brain. Eventually, all the nerve endings meet and bond seamlessly.

THE BUILT-IN PHARMACY

Next time you go to the drug store, stand in front of the counter for a minute and take a good look. The shelves are lined with bottles of hundreds of different medicines. Each one was developed to simulate something that a healthy body does on its own! A healthy person needs no medicine. His body automatically performs the task that the medicine was designed to perform in a body that is malfunctioning. The blood pressure is just right and needs no adjustment. The heart beat is as it should be and does not need to be regulated. The body produces sufficient insulin to process the glucose in the bloodstream. Each one of these medicines was researched and developed over years. It was tested over and over again to make sure it did the job. The body just does all this automatically, with no need for research or laboratory experiments.

---

53 The technical name is ductus arteriosus.

CHAPTER EIGHTEEN

A Deeper Look

Up until now, we have spoken mostly about things that can be seen even with a superficial look. Now we will give a sampling of the deeper complexities that have recently been revealed by modern science. Not so long ago, the schools taught us about the "simple cell." Each individual cell in the body was considered very simple. It was a little bit of protoplasm, a nucleus and a membrane around the cell. Now the scientists know that each cell has more activity going on inside it than a major metropolis like New York City or London! There are endless factories that produce hundreds of different types of proteins needed for the body. As we have just quoted, each cell contains a DNA molecule. It is a genetic code of instructions for this and every other cell in the body. If these complicated instructions were to be written out, they would fill thousands of thick volumes. Staggering!

The following excerpt was taken from a book called *What Darwin Didn't Know*. It was written by a (non-Jewish) doctor by the name of Geoffrey Simmons. This doctor describes, in chapter after chapter, the complexities of every system in the human body. He contends that it is unthinkable that all this complexity evolved by a series of unguided, lucky accidents, and must have been guided by some infinite intelligence.

An Excerpt from *What Darwin Didn't Know*[54]
The Genes

> *Everything that transpires within the body is controlled by the three billion base pairs that make up the 100,000 genes that form the twenty-three paired chromosomes within the nucleus of nearly every cell. The amount of information stored within a single nucleus is equal to a library of 1,000 encyclopedias, each with 1,000 pages. Multiply that by the thirty-five billion cells in a brain, not to mention the ten or more trillion cells in the body, and the amount of information moving about the body in each second becomes astronomical. Yet if one could put all of the DNA coordinating the growth, development, and functioning of every human on earth into a single pile, it would weigh barely fifty grams. How could a particle smaller than dust have enough knowledge to, as it were, multiply into a trillion room skyscraper — and also know the color, shape and size of every room, every worker who would ever be employed in it and every speck of furniture, wiring and plumbing? (This speck might even know the past, present and the future.)*
>
> *Did these all-knowing genes come about through a series of accidents? If so, that would mean that an average of two bases were added to our chromosomes per year throughout the presumed three billion years of life. They were also placed in the right order at the right time on the correct chromosomes, and were fully capable of coordinating with the other genes. For example, the genes that control human eye color and shape must either reside close by each other or have a way of communicating. The gene specifying the texture of a person's hair would not function well if it were placed with the genes for the ear or for bladder function. A major challenge to evolution has been whether repeated mutations could truly change in the correct order.*

The complexity of the human brain is nothing less than astounding. The brain is connected to every part of your body by nerve fibers which bring electronic impulses to and from the brain. When you put your hand on something warm or wet, the nerve endings in your fingers send a message to the brain. The brain searches through its archives containing trillions of pieces of information, and identifies what your hand is feeling and whether it

---

54   Geoffrey Simmons, M.D., *What Darwin Didn't Know* (Harvest House Publishers, 2004), p. 30.

is dangerous or not. It sends its response within less than a split second. This system is far more complex than all the telecommunication systems in the world today. How could this possibly have come about through some gradual development over millions of years? The following is an excerpt from a book written by an eminent (non-Jewish) scientist, Michael Denton, PhD, who concludes that the theory of evolution cannot possibly be correct.

An Excerpt from *Evolution: A Theory in Crisis*

> *In terms of complexity, an individual cell is nothing when compared with a system like the mammalian brain. The human brain consists of about ten thousand million nerve cells. Each nerve cell puts out between ten thousand and one hundred thousand connecting fibers by which it makes contact with other nerve cells in the brain. Altogether the total number of connections in the human brain approaches 10^{15} or a thousand million million. Numbers in the order of 10^{15} are of course completely beyond comprehension. Imagine an area about half the size of the USA (one million square miles) covered in a forest of trees containing ten thousand trees per square mile. If each tree contained one hundred thousand leaves, the total number of leaves in the forest would be 10^{15} — equivalent to the number of connections in the human brain! Despite the enormity of the number of connections, the ramifying forest of fibers is not a chaotic random tangle but is a highly organized network in which a high proportion of the fibers are unique adaptive communication channels following their own specially ordained pathway through the brain. Even if only one hundredth of the connections in the brain were specifically organized, this would still represent a system containing a much greater number of specific connections than in the entire communications network on earth.*[55]

OUR FIVE SENSES

Humans have been endowed with five senses: sight, hearing, smell, taste and touch. Even a paragraph or two about the marvels of each one of these senses is grossly inadequate. Each one could be a subject unto itself. All five

---

55 Michael Denton, *Evolution: A Theory in Crisis*, 1985, p. 330.

A Deeper Look

are sufficiently complex to stagger the imagination, and fill us with awe of the infinite intelligence that brought them into being. Here again, we refer to the wonderful book, *What Darwin Didn't Know*, taking only a small excerpt from an entire chapter about each of the five senses.

SIGHT

> "Millions of cells lining the interior of each eye function as photo-chemical receivers that convert light waves into a myriad of electrical impulses, which are forwarded, at a speed of about 200 miles per hour, to the brain — and then sorted, organized and analyzed. This is accomplished in milliseconds... Note that both eyes, unless damaged, move in perfect unison...Our eyes are kept moist and nearly sterile by tiny lacrimal glands along the outer edge of each upper eyelid...This same fluid also brings oxygen to the cornea — which cannot have vision-blocking blood vessels on its surface — and brings proteins to coat the eye. Is that accidental or design?...Blinking is another protective function which we do about 14,000 to 20,000 times a day."

HEARING

> The sound waves "ricochet down the outer canal to the eardrum, set up vibrations that are passed through three tiny bones in the middle ear, called the hammer, anvil and stirrup, to a fluid-filled apparatus called the cochlea. Ripples in the cochlea's fluid stimulate hair cells. Envision fields of hay swaying with numerous and varied gusts of wind.
>
> The inner hair cells do most of the hearing, while the outer hair cells do most of the fine-tuning. Each ear has about 35,000 inner hair cells and 20,000 outer hair cells, and each of these have between fifty and a hundred stereocilia, or tiny hairs. The information they sense is changed into electrical impulses that combine to form the acoustic nerve going to the brain."

SMELL

> "The six million olfactory (smelling) cells inside a nose can detect 10,000 separate odors and up to a half-million combination odors. We can diagnose disease, detect danger, identify food, recognize relatives...with our noses... Air is filtered by small hairs as it is inhaled by the expanding lungs. This protects us from pollen, dander, dust, bacteria, fungi, viruses, smog... The shape of the nose is important. This shape utilizes the same principle as the ears, capturing aromas and funneling them inside to a complex, more protected area for analysis."

TASTE

> If you stand in front of a mirror and stick your tongue far out "you might see a V-shaped pattern of larger, button-like growths across the very back. The papillae contain most of our 10,000 taste buds...The tongue can stretch forward to taste with a lick. It can sense if a bone is present, ferret out unwanted matter, scrape bits of food away from crevices between teeth, help form words, sense the temperature of food, help digest food by secreting enzymes, initiate the swallowing process and help spit out bad food."

TOUCH

> A network of millions of sensory receptors blankets every square millimeter of the human body. It is designed to help us carry out every function, to protect us and give us pleasure...Sensory receptors come in a variety of shapes and sizes. Many act like tiny frayed electrical wires, ready to fire off the instant they are touched. Meissner corpuscles... are located between the epidermis and the dermis. ...Every fingertip has about 9,000 of these corpuscles (sensory receptors) per square inch. They can distinguish between different types of light touch, between sharp and dull, between various textures; they can detect low frequency vibrations and the size of any stimulus."

Could any sensible person attribute all these arrangements to a series of unguided natural processes? The infinite intelligence and design is blatantly obvious.

PART FOUR

EVOLUTION — YOU BE THE JUDGE

CHAPTER NINETEEN

The Essence of the Theory

Although some readers may be familiar with the theory of evolution, others may not be. So here we will present the basic idea of this theory. It cannot be emphasized enough how important it is to understand what this theory really implies. Then we will be able to judge properly whether it makes any sense or not.

The theory of evolution was popularized in the world by a naturalist named Charles Darwin. Darwin did not address, and indeed had no idea, how the first life came into existence. His theory starts from the point when there was, supposedly, nothing more than a simple organism (perhaps a single cell). From this organism, he postulated, everything else gradually evolved. All living things (plants, insects, animal, humans, etc.) descend from this common ancestor. With the passage of eons of time, this simple organism produced offspring with very, very slight modifications. Darwin never addressed, and had no idea, how those modifications came to be. The modification that was positive and beneficial enabled that branch of the family to survive better than others without it. This is called "survival of the fittest," and the process of eliminating the weaker strains and keeping the stronger ones is known as "natural selection." These modifications happened ever so slowly, taking very numerous steps, but eventually new organs and even new species came into being by these processes.

According to Darwinians, amphibians came from fish, reptiles from amphibians, birds came from reptiles, and whales from a common ancestor of what is now the hippopotamus. It certainly requires a considerable stretch of the imagination.

NEO-DARWINISM

Darwin knew nothing about genes and genetics. He thought that the cell is a simple glob of protoplasm.[56] In the 1930s, the scientists had to adjust the theory to be compatible with the new knowledge of genetics.

This is what they said then, and it is currently the most popularly accepted version of the theory: Evolution's gradual steps that produce numerous small changes, which eventually add up to major changes, are caused by sudden random mutations, or errors, in the genes. This is how, for example, a creature that once had no wings developed wings. Even though most changes by gene mutations are negative (harmful), sometimes a change can be positive. Thousands of small changes were necessary to make the transition from no wings to wings (or to develop some other body part or species which had not existed before). Each of these changes needed to be integrated into the whole body system. Then natural selection took over. Those that had not developed in this manner were not as capable of survival as the others. They died out in time. That is why we see only the successful ones and not the failures. This is called survival of the fittest. That, in a nutshell, is the essence of the current version of the theory of evolution.

Please note that Darwin wrote in a letter that, in his opinion, the theory of evolution circumvents the necessity for belief in a Creator. According to the theory, everything in existence came about without any intelligent force guiding it or controlling it. The trees, the animals, the heart and the lungs, etc. all resulted through totally unguided and natural processes.

"If I were convinced that I required such additions to the theory of natural selection, I would reject it as rubbish... I would give nothing for

---

56 Scientists now know that the complexity of even the simplest organism staggers the imagination. We have already discussed DNA.

the theory of natural selection, if it requires miraculous additions at any one stage of descent."[57]

In previous chapters, we spoke at length about the astounding miracles of nature. Each one demonstrates cunning plan and purpose. Each creature has all the instincts, tools and accessories it needs for its existence. Every organ is precision-made to fulfill its function. The theory, however, recognizes no intelligence whatsoever in any living things. Although it does not seem plausible for anyone to suggest that all of this came about by a series of random gene mutations with no intelligence behind them, this is indeed what they are saying. This is key to the issue. The impression that scientists often give is that the proofs are incontrovertible, but the matter is not quite so simple.

IN BRIEF

Just to summarize briefly, the theory states:

- That all living things come from a simple one-celled common ancestor.
- That all the complex organisms, the countless species and the organized systems that are in existence came about by unguided natural processes, with no intelligence behind them.
- Neo-Darwinism adds that the mechanism for bringing about those changes is gene mutations, which means mistakes in the copying process of the genes.

HOW IT SEEMS TO US

Although evolutionists will declare vehemently that these are totally natural processes, common sense dictates that this is equivalent to saying it all happened by chance. The necessary random mutations didn't have to occur. They didn't all have to fit neatly together to work in harmony

---

57 Richard Dawkins, *The Blind Watchmaker* (University of Oxford). "In Darwin's view the whole point of the theory of evolution by natural selection was that it provided a non-miraculous account of the existence of complex adaptations... For Darwin, any evolution that had to be helped over the jumps by G-d was not evolution at all."

with the rest of the body's systems. The mathematical odds against such a thing happening even once are astronomical, but we are being told that it happened billions of times. Thus, it is by plain sheer luck that there exist now fins, feathers, arms, legs, a heart, a liver and lungs in creatures whose ancestors had none. No intelligence worked out the details of the highly complicated respiratory, digestive and nervous systems. Where did they all come from? An endless series of random mutations (mistakes in the genes), each one gradually complementing the others until they arrived, over the course of a few million (or billion) years, at the finished product.

ON WHOM IS THE BURDEN OF PROOF?

Before we even begin, you must know that the burden of proof rests on the evolutionists, not on us. As we have already shown, the evidence of an infinite intelligence is everywhere we turn. Is it we who have to prove that the human brain, with more connections than all the telecommunication systems in the world, displays a vast intelligence, or they who have to show that such an ingeniously complex machine can develop through natural unguided processes?

CHAPTER TWENTY

A Common Sense Approach

*I*t is important for the reader to know what we are attempting to do in this section of our book. This is not a scientific work. I take the position of a high school or university student confronted with the evidence presented in the textbooks and popularized by the media. After all, these are the mediums through which public opinion has been swayed toward belief in the theory of evolution. We will quote some of the (so-called) scientific proofs that are offered to substantiate the theory, and scrutinize the material and see if it adds up. We will make the reader aware that there are serious problems here, quote some statements from the scientists about their own difficulties with the theory,[58] and then appeal to the reader's common sense. Let him come to an initial judgment himself. I have deliberately tried to simplify the material here, address the material that appears on the surface, and try to make it understandable for laymen like myself, regardless of age.[59]

---

58 Most of them will never forsake the theory, no matter how many overwhelming problems they encounter. However, very many express strong disapproval, some with one proof, others with another. Every proof has eminent scientists, even from among those faithful to the theory, that reject the particular proof.

59 These issues are particularly confusing for teenagers and young adults.

Of course, the scientists will defend themselves against criticism, and the critics will claim that their defenses are ridiculous. Anyone who feels the need to pursue the matter further is invited, by all means, to do so.[60] What we will have accomplished is to have made the honest objective seeker aware of the basic problems. We maintain that it is not necessary to be a scientist to see that the theory is not commensurate with the dictates of plain common sense. For this, however, we will let the reader be the judge.

AN ESTABLISHED FACT?

School textbooks and the media present the theory of evolution as something that has been so firmly demonstrated that it can be considered a fact, as well established as the concept that the earth is round and not flat. Most laypeople are indeed under the impression that this is so. They have a confidence — a sort of *emunah peshutah* — in the scientific consensus, assuming that all has been objectively researched and proved beyond a shadow of a doubt. They have heard it in school and they've read it in the media. We hope to demonstrate that this confidence is very far from justified. First and foremost, we maintain that the theory flies in the face of plain common sense. If indeed that is the case, a person will approach all the so-called "proofs" that are offered with a suspicious eye, realizing that there is likely some mistake here, because it just doesn't make sense. If, under further investigation, we see that there are actually severe problems with the theory, and flaws in their proofs, we will become all the more skeptical.

NOT BY VOTE

There is a tendency to become overwhelmed by the large numbers and sophisticated credentials of the scientists who subscribe to the theory of evolution. People think to themselves, "All these highly educated people can't be wrong." There are a number of things to bear in mind

---

60 For those that feel they need to see the arguments and counter arguments in their original format, they certainly can pursue this further. We believe that, for many, what is written here will suffice to convince them that this is a pursuit after falsehood and foolishness.

here. Perhaps there is an impression that there is unanimous acceptance of this theory. That is simply not the case. There is an entire body of eminent scientists[61] who reject this theory completely, and declare that all the "proofs" are not conclusive. Many of these favor what they call "intelligent design." This means that the complexity of such things as coded information in the DNA, molecular machinery, the mammalian brain and the fine tuning in the laws of Nature can best be explained by attributing it to a vast intelligence.[62]

These experts have written many books in an attempt to refute the theory. The credentials of these authors are at least equal to those of their opponents. Although they may not be the majority, the decision of evolution versus intelligent design/creation must not be dependent upon a vote. The opinion of the scientists who reject evolution is just as reliable as the opinion of those who support it. Certainly, no sensible judgment can be made on this matter until hearing both sides thoroughly. Because the leftist elite in the media and the universities favor evolution, they will almost never present the other side accurately. The textbooks and the media support evolution. High schools and universities teach it as if it were fact. Governments, too, support the theory. In many states in the United States it is against the law to teach students that there is an alternative to evolution. There have been major court cases about this, and the evolutionists have won the day. The courts' decision is based on the excuse that there must be "a separation of Church and state." This means that the government cannot sanction any religious belief. From teaching Intelligent Design, which does not officially discuss a Creator, students might get the terrible idea that there is a G-d. Hence, in essence, atheism is now the national religion of the United States. But media and state governments are not the ones to decide matters of *emunah*.

Furthermore, not all the scientists who jump on the evolutionary bandwagon are experts in evolution per se. Not all of them did the

---

61 There is a website called "Dissent from Darwin Blog" which lists about a thousand distinguished scientists (and their positions) who do not subscribe to the theory of evolution.

62 This doesn't necessarily mean that all these scientists believe in Hashem, but at least they admit that the world had to have a master designer. We, on the other hand, know precisely Who that designer is.

research or made the measurements that might lead them to accept the theory. They, too, were trained by the high school and university textbooks, which present only a very biased one-sided view of the issue. They subscribe to evolution, just as the masses of laymen do, because it is popularly accepted by the majority of their peers who specialize in those fields. Therefore, we advise, don't be impressed by numbers or credentials. Neither numbers nor credentials will decide this matter. First engage your own common sense. You may see, even before entering the discussion of the evolutionists' arguments, that evolution is simply not believable. Upon further scrutiny, you may conclude that the arguments of the pro-evolutionists do not add up, and that two plus two does not equal five.[63]

Numbers mean nothing. Christianity and Islam are mutually exclusive. Each system has more than a billion adherents. Among these adherents are many brilliant people with PhDs and all kinds of fancy credentials: doctors, lawyers, accountants, philosophers, theologians and professors. Each group claims that the other will burn in hell for eternity. Yet one of these groups containing all those brilliant minds must have made an error, because these two are mutually exclusive. If the one is true, the other is automatically false.[64] Therefore, instead of counting the numbers of those who believe in the theory, engage your own common sense first. When the truth is clear to you, then you can try to figure out how and why so many can be in error.

PROPAGANDA

Most people have been exposed to the writings of the evolutionists, in school or in the media. Considerably fewer have ever been exposed to the presentation of the other side. Such people may not even be aware that there are any problems with the theory at all. However, there certainly are, but these are almost never presented to high school or even university students. Some of these are very glaring problems, which school textbooks prefer to hush up, because the proponents of the theory would then be put on the defensive.

---

63 We will yet present why we believe that they are indeed telling us that two plus two equals five.
64 Of course, we are certain that both groups are in serious error, but that is not our subject right now.

Do not be surprised that most of the world accepts all this as if it were proved and axiomatic. If someone has read only material in favor of evolution, he has been propagandized. Hitler, *yemach shemo*, told his propaganda minister Goebels, *yemach shemo*, "It makes no difference what you say. Just keep repeating it enough times and eventually they will believe it." The minds of the masses have been conditioned to the words, adapted, evolved and developed, to the point that all this seems perfectly logical to them. This is due to the massive torrent of propaganda in favor of the theory.

THE STORY OF LARRY

Larry was a secular Jew who worked as a technician for Bell Telephone. He came to his first Torah class ever, and after the class we sat down to talk. Larry said, "There's one thing that it doesn't pay to speak about. That's evolution. Evolution is in my bloodstream." I responded, "There are plenty of other things to discuss. We can avoid the evolution subject altogether." Of course, we wound up discussing evolution. After half an hour Larry said, "This is incredible. I don't believe in evolution anymore." I told him that it's not at all surprising. No one in Communist Russia ever lost an election. (There was never more than one candidate.) "All your life you heard only one side. Now that you've finally heard the other side, you don't subscribe to evolution anymore."[65] Propaganda works wonders on people.

DON'T BE IMPRESSED

Theories come and theories go. There are dozens of examples of fundamental scientific beliefs that were universally agreed upon, until new research forced the scientific community to change its mind. Up until quite recently, scientists believed in a static universe, which means that it had always existed, with no beginning. It was considered axiomatic that the universe had always been there. Subsequent research introduced the Big Bang, which means that the universe had a beginning.[66] Today, the Big Bang is almost universally accepted.

---

65 Today, Larry is Leibel, a *sofer* in Yerushalayim.

66 Much to the chagrin of many scientists, as we shall discuss later.

The theory of evolution, as well, is very different today than what Darwin proposed. They have altered and changed it multiple times, and it has gone through numerous phases.

Generally, the believers in evolution don't ever give up on the theory itself. No matter how many problems they encounter, they persist in their acceptance of evolution. They do, however, argue about the various proofs. None of them are ironclad. Every proof has opponents, even among the staunchest adherents of evolution.

A very basic rule in science is that in order to prove something you need empirical proof. Empirical proof means that we can observe the evidence to prove the theory. You can see it happen, or test it in a laboratory. In order to get a new medicine approved for marketing, endless experiments must be done to show that it works and has no harmful side effects. We intend to show that, despite their claims, evolution has no empirical proof whatsoever that the mechanism of gene mutations can produce such wonders as wings, eyes and the mammalian brain. No new type of living thing has evolved in human experience. In spite of the fact that a good part of the world considers it a documented fact, this idea is not more than a theory, and a very problematic one at that.

CHAPTER TWENTY-ONE

Glaring Problems

When viewed with an objective eye, the matter is not the way it has been presented to the general public at all. Let's view the theory under a magnifying glass, with a skeptical eye, and see things the way they really are.

A VARIETY OF ISSUES

As we will see, there are a number of different elements in the problems with the theory:

1. Much of the logic on which the theory is based simply does not hold water.
2. Under scrutiny, the observable facts do not indicate what they want to prove.
3. There are facts that are withheld from the general public in the textbooks and media.
4. Discarded evidence is still being used in the textbooks and media.
5. In some instances, there is an element of outright deception.

THE LOGIC DOESN'T HOLD WATER

Just how small is the probability for one organ to have just the right gene mutations to turn into something more complex? Don't forget, not only do its body and organ structure have to be completely re-organized, the DNA also has to undergo all the necessary changes. All components of the new organ or new species, and all the body systems, have to work as a unified whole for the benefit of the organism. The chances of that happening are so infinitesimally small, that they are actually nil.[67]

The lame excuse, "given enough time, anything can happen," just won't cut it. Imagine shooting one hundred dice and waiting to see how long it would take for all one hundred to land with all the number six sides facing up. It is highly improbable, the odds against it are astronomical, but it could happen. Since the dice always fall randomly, they might one time fall with all one hundred sixes facing up. But you can shoot those dice a trillion times and they will never turn into potato chips. The idea that fish can turn into amphibians, amphibians into reptiles, and reptiles into birds is simply an unacceptable stretch of the imagination. As we will yet see, evolution of one new organism, one wing etc., has never been witnessed even once in recorded history.

They are actually saying much more than just the idea that the millions of types of plants and living creatures evolved from a common ancestor. In order for the changes to be passed on in the genes, they must postulate that every single one of the thousands (or millions) of mutations required to get from one species to another was beneficial to the organism. This suggestion, too, staggers the imagination.

Attributing to these changes a mechanism of gene mutations (or any other mechanism) does not detract one iota from the frivolity of the theory. Natural selection does not create anything. It just weeds out the ones that are less fit to survive. The changes come about (according to the theory) by random mutations. This still boils down to accident; gradual development with no intelligence behind it. They

---

67 If someone were to try to shuffle fifteen sheets of paper numbered one to fifteen, the chance of them falling randomly into the correct order is one chance in 1,307,700,000,000. Any new organ is considerably more complicated than that. (*Rejoice O Youth*, paragraph 27).

admit that most mutations are not helpful or positive. No mutation in recorded history has ever produced a new organ,[68] and certainly not a new plant, insect, reptile, bird or any other creature. There certainly is no reason to assume that any second mutation should complement the first (or the ten thousandth and first should complement the ten thousandth). These thousands times thousands of mutations all have to fit together, like the pieces of a gigantic jigsaw puzzle. They all need to work in harmony for the benefit of the organism. After all, the scientists themselves are forced to admit that gene mutations are just accidents. So, it is an accident that there are muscles, bones, kidneys and eyes. The brain, the eyes and the circulatory system all just somehow happened to happily evolve!

SURVIVAL OF THE UNFIT

According to the theory, each of the gradual changes somehow enabled the species to survive better than the same species that did not experience that particular change. These were the "fittest" and the rule called "survival of the fittest" applied to them.

The logic does not seem to add up. Although evolutionists will insist that every small change brought some improvement into the organism, it is difficult to imagine how the organism functioned before the evolutionary process was completed. For example, when we look at lungs today, every component is necessary for the process of respiration. Without any one of these components, the whole machinery would serve no purpose. If it took millions of years for lungs to develop in a species that had no lungs before, then that organ would have been useless for respiration until the final stages of development. How did the species breathe all that time? With all their fertile powers of imagination, evolutionists have produced no convincing detailed Darwinian pathways for any organ of organized complexity.

---

68   Mutations can cause extra organs, such as an extra human finger or extra wings on fruit flies. But there is no recorded case where an intrinsically new organ, such as a lung or a brain where there was none before, was caused by a gene mutation.

Glaring Problems   179

A QUOTE FROM A THEORY IN CRISIS

> *"Just how such an utterly different respiratory system could have evolved gradually from the standard vertebrate design is fantastically difficult to envisage, especially bearing in mind that the maintenance of respiratory function is absolutely vital to the life of an organism to the extent that the slightest malfunction leads to death within minutes. Just as the feather cannot function as an organ of flight until the hooks and barbules are coadapted to fit together perfectly, so the avian lung cannot function as an organ of respiration until the parabronchi system which permeates it and the air sac system which guarantees the parabronchi their air supply are both highly developed and able to function together in a perfectly integrated manner."*[69]

HOW DID LIFE BEGIN?

The prevalent theory does not resolve a major issue: Where did the original life come from? Can life arise spontaneously? For years they had been glibly telling us that the first life must have arisen spontaneously from some "chemical soup" which covered the earth eons ago. Somehow there was a chemical reaction, and poof! — there was the first living thing. Not only was that simple single cell alive, but it even had the ability to reproduce. Scientists now know that reproduction needs DNA. Was there actually ready-made DNA in that very first cell? Scientists, with all their technological know-how and sophisticated equipment, are unable to recreate any sort of life in the laboratory. They certainly have never seen any spontaneous life come into existence. The current scientific community generally admits that they have no idea how life could have arisen spontaneously, and they realize that the possibility of it happening is highly unlikely.

It is important to remember that the scientific establishment itself has a totally different perception of even the simplest form of life than it had fifty or sixty years ago. When I went to school, we were taught

---

69   Michael Denton, *A Theory in Crisis* (Adler & Adler, 1986), pp. 211–212.

about the simple cell. Living things are made up of many individual cells. They taught us that each cell was understood to be nothing more than a glob of jelly with a nucleus in the middle and a membrane around the edge. Now they know that even the simplest cell is more complex than we can imagine.

Yet many, as an article of faith, are still convinced that spontaneous generation actually did happen, although they fail to offer any explanation as to how it could have happened. This is a problem for which they have no solution as yet. Yet they are forced to say it happened somehow, because otherwise they will have no choice but to believe in a Creator.

BIG BANG

A question similar to how the first life began can also be applied to the Big Bang theory. Big Bang theory states that the entire universe started when some condensed material exploded, began expanding outward, and continues to expand right up to the present. Although the Big Bang brings us (and the scientists) much closer to *Bereishis* than the previous belief in a static universe, most of the scientists who subscribe to the belief in Big Bang have not yet come to admit the existence of the Creator.

According to them, the big question remains unresolved. If they admit that the entire universe came about through this Big Bang, then where did the original substance that exploded come from? How did that original substance contain all the materials that would eventually turn into a universe, replete with stars, planets, trees, plants and animals? This question is so obvious, yet it seems to get overlooked. Without resorting to the belief in a Creator, there are currently no answers to these questions. It is logical to say with certainty that there never will be.

INFORMATION WITHOUT INTELLIGENCE?

How did information get programmed into the DNA? How does the Darwinian mechanism account for the astounding coded information and organized complexity in the DNA of the cell? In all human experience, information always indicates intelligence.

CHAPTER TWENTY-TWO

Some Things Just Don't Add Up

*E*volutionists present various proofs to demonstrate that evolution has taken place, and that the theory is the correct explanation for the existence of all the complicated phenomena of nature. They present their findings and confidently declare that these findings leave us no option but to conclude that evolution is true. Although the evidence they present may (sometimes) be factual, the conclusions they draw from that evidence leave us altogether startled.

LITTLE DOES NOT EQUAL BIG

All recorded cases of (so-called) evolution that scientists cite as proof are only minor changes within the species. Scientists generally call such changes "microevolution." Darwin's book was called *Origin of the Species*. He claimed that from gradual minor changes, one species is able to change into another. Scientists generally call these larger changes "macroevolution." That is how he explained the millions of different types of creatures in the world, with all their various organs. In order to demonstrate that the theory is correct, one would have to cite examples of gradual development, progressing from one stage to the next in minor increments, until finally one species turned into another, or (at least) a new organ developed in a species that had no such organ before. There is not one single example of this to point to. All the examples of so-called evolution demonstrate only minor changes within the given species. The following three examples are icons of evolution, found in almost every textbook that deals with the subject.

BACTERIAL RESISTANCE TO ANTIBIOTICS

Although antibiotics can destroy harmful bacteria, experiments have shown that bacteria can develop a resistance to antibiotics. To the scientists, this is an astounding example of evolution at work, a stunning example of how a species can evolve. Previously, the bacteria were killed by the antibiotics, now they have evolved into a new strain of bacteria that are resistant to the antibiotics — evolution!

Two plus two does not equal five. Bacteria that have developed a resistance to antibiotics are nothing more than bacteria. There is neither a new organ nor a new species here. This is no proof at all that a new organ or a new creature can develop through evolution. The genes of any given organism may indeed have sufficient flexibility to make certain changes within the parameters of the species, but always remain the same basic species. How can this be presented as a proof that one species can evolve into another? As we will see, all the major examples of evolution are similar in this respect. (This is a major point of refutation). They've never seen it happen even once, but they expect us to accept that it happened billions of times.

GALAPAGOS FINCHES

In a time of drought, some finches on the Galapagos Islands developed larger beaks. The evolutionists claim that when there was a shortage of food and the finches needed larger beaks to crack open nuts, evolution enabled them to develop such beaks. Now they were able to crack open certain thick-shelled nuts to supplement their food source, and survive the shortage caused by the drought. Scientists point to these changes in the size of the Galapagos finches' beaks and tell us that we have witnessed evolution! However, this is no proof at all! A finch with a (slightly) bigger beak is exactly the same bird as the finch with the smaller beak. They can (and do) mate together as one species.[70] This does not prove what they are setting out to prove, that new organs and species can come about through evolution.

PEPPERED MOTHS

Evolutionists cite the case of the peppered moths as an example of evolution. The peppered moth, native to England, is a white moth covered with a sprinkling of black spots that look like ground pepper. This is their claim: The peppered moths roost on the trunks of trees, and were camouflaged by the lichens growing on the trees. During the Industrial Revolution, the trees became covered with black soot. Against the black background, the peppered moths could easily be seen by the birds that eat them. Now most of the moths are colored black as a result of evolution. Conclusive proof!

The flaw in this argument is the same as in the two previous ones. A moth with peppered spots is no different than a black moth. No new organ or species has evolved.[71] The "origin of the species" has not been demonstrated in the slightest.[72]

---

70   If a finch can develop a larger beak, does that mean that a bear can turn into a whale? (Darwin actually made such a ridiculous statement.)

71   We have granted the scientists the benefit of the doubt that there was some microevolution here in the finches and the peppered moths. This is, however, not certain at all. There were always some finches with larger beaks. Only the proportion of the finch population changed in response to the drought. Likewise, there always existed moths with the peppered coloring and moths with all black coloring. Only the proportions changed. Where is the evolution?

72   We shall yet return to the finches and peppered moths. There are more significant problems with these "proofs" than what has been presented so far.

CHAPTER TWENTY-THREE

Fossils

One of the pillars upon which the theory stands is the fossil record. For those unfamiliar with this, we will try to define what that means. Under certain conditions, the remains of creatures that have died turn into rock-like substance, and we can see the whole outline of that creature as it was when it was alive. Hidden in the earth or in the rocks, we find the fossilized remains of creatures, some of which no longer exist.

The general impression that students walk away with is that fossils are automatically an indication of antiquity, and that these fossils come from an era hundreds of thousands or even millions of years ago. Seldom will the high school or university student hear that fossils have been found that can be clearly identified as being of very recent origin. This means that just because something has been fossilized, it is not necessarily any indication that it is very old.

MISSING LINKS

For decades, the theorists have claimed that the strongest evidence for the theory of evolution is to be found in the fossil record. However, there are some facts about fossils that students will probably never be taught in school.

According to the theory, fish evolved into amphibians, amphibians into reptiles and reptiles into mammals. Therefore, just as we find fossilized remains of these categories, we ought to find fossilized remains of all the stages in between when (for example) the fish was part fish and part amphibian. There ought to be multitudes of fossils of the "intermediate stages" and of the species that evolved in ways that made them unfit for survival. Where are all the missing sequences of transitional fossils? Where are the fossils of the failures?

Darwin was very disappointed that the "missing links" had not been found. He was confident that the reason was that they simply had not yet unearthed enough fossils. With the passage of time and more digging, he was sure they would be found. About 150 years of constant digging have gone by and still there are no missing links. Most authorities have given up hope of their being discovered and seek "other explanations" as to why they are not where they ought to be. Some diehards still cling to the hope that they will be found.

However, common sense dictates that if:

- the scientists say that everything evolved from lower to higher, and
- there are countless fossils of the major stages, (fish, amphibian, reptile and mammal), then
- there ought to be fossils of all the transitory (in-between) stages which, according to the theory, must have existed, and
- if they are absent, it is the clearest evidence that they never existed, and that all species existed side by side from the beginning.

Hence, not only does the fossil record not constitute the greatest proof of evolution, it is the greatest proof against evolution! Sometimes, in a moment of honesty, the experts admit the truth about the fossils. Just consider this quote from evolutionary microbiologist James Shapiro of the University of Chicago: "There are no detailed Darwinian accounts for the evolution of any fundamental biochemical or cellular systems, only a variety of wishful speculations."[73]

---

73   In a review of *Darwin's Black Box: The Biochemical Challenge to Evolution* by Michael Behe, *National Review*, pp. 62–65, September 1996.

TRANSITIONAL FOSSILS

When the scientists find fossils that have some features similar to species they consider "earlier," and some features similar to species that they consider "later," they declare them transitional fossils. The assumption is that these "in-betweens" evolved from the former, and the latter evolved from them. One of their favorite examples is called archaeopteryx, which has some features of dinosaurs and some features of birds. For example, this creature had teeth and a long bony tale (which birds do not have), and feathers (which dinosaurs did not have). As a result, they concluded that modern day birds have evolved from dinosaurs. Even from a secular standpoint this is merely conjecture. A single organism with some features of this and some features of that does not make it a transitional fossil. However, let us not forget that if their thinking is correct, there ought to be very numerous "transitional fossils" in graded sequence from the dinosaur to the bird. The absence of those fossils constitutes considerably stronger evidence against the theory than the conjecture that they have found a single transitional fossil.

Larry Martin is considered one of the world's foremost experts on the birds of the Mesozoic era, which is when the archaeopteryx supposedly lived. While reviewing a book critical of the bird-dinosaur connection, he wrote the following amazing statement:

> "I began to grow disenchanted with the bird-dinosaur link when I compared the eighty-five or so anatomical features seriously proposed as being shared by birds and dinosaurs. To my shock, virtually none of the comparisons held up. The moral of the story is that such poor attention to detail has been repeated with almost every feature cited to support a bird-dinosaur relation. No wonder that this book has an undercurrent of righteous outrage."

Transitional fossils prove nothing.

HOMOLOGY

One of the major proofs to the theory is from something called homology. Homology means that we assume that creatures with similar body or bone structures must have come from a common ancestor. How else would they share similar bone shapes or body parts? Scientists feel that if they can show similarity in limbs or bone structure, it is a proof that all these creatures must have descended from a common ancestor.

This, however, is a very weak proof. There are many examples of things that have similar features, but about which it is universally agreed upon that they did not descend from a recent common ancestor. The giant panda and the red panda, both native to China, have similar thumbs. Although there was much discussion about this, the experts have concluded that the two are not closely related at all. The giant panda is considered to be a member of the bear family, while the red panda is a member of the raccoon family. Yet they have exactly the same type of panda thumb.[74] Obviously, just because things look similar is no proof whatsoever that they evolved one from the other, or from a common ancestor.

The reader realizes, of course, that the belief in a Creator explains homology just as well, if not much better, than common ancestry. The infinitely intelligent Designer used the same design and features in many different models He created, just as, *l'havdil*, the car manufacturer puts many similar features, but not all, into the different models of cars he designs.

CAMBRIAN EXPLOSION

Then there is the problem of the Cambrian explosion. The geologists divide the history of the world into periods and postulate in which period the various species evolved. The Cambrian is one of these periods. The fossils found in what they consider the Cambrian contain the majority of body designs existing in our world today. The strata beneath the Cambrian do not contain the fossils which the theory dictates should have preceded the fossils in the Cambrian. The scientists refer to this as having "appeared suddenly" in the fossil record. This has been acknowledged by all authorities to be a major problem with the theory.[75]

---

74 See Yoram Bogacz, *Genesis and Genes* (2013), p. 190, for many more homological similarities between these two animals, in spite of their not having descended from a recent common ancestor.

75 As we will see later, even such a major problem does not make them lose faith in the theory. Many top evolutionists declare their adherence to the theory against all odds. It is a case of *emunah peshutah* at its best.

CHAPTER TWENTY-FOUR

More Proofs

The theorists claim that their position is substantiated from many different branches of science, with various conclusive proofs. Let's take a look at a few more, and see how convincing they really are.

VESTIGIAL ORGANS

One of the classical proofs that evolutionists bring is from what they call "vestigial organs." Supposedly, the scientists have identified organs in the human body (or in animals) that have relatively little or no function. Hence, they deduce that these organs are the remainders of some previous evolutionary stage. Their list of these organs was very long. It is very easy to arrogantly declare an organ useless when one does not know its function. One by one, researchers discovered that each of these organs does indeed serve some purpose, often a vital one at that. Their list has grown considerably smaller.

Tonsils were considered to be a useless organ, and since it was easy to operate on them, doctors would remove them regularly if they seemed to be inflamed. Two million tonsillectomies were performed in the United

States every year.[76] Now it is known that tonsils play a very important role in protecting the body from infection. The encyclopedia says, "The tonsils function as the first outpost of the body's immune defense system." Another quotation: "[The tonsils are] two lumps of tissue that work as germ fighters."

The pituitary gland was also assumed to be one of these vestigial organs. Doctors would have operated on it too, but it is too difficult to reach, so they left it in. It is currently known that the pituitary is the master gland in the body. Although they keep knocking items off the list, the idea has not yet penetrated that everything in the body and everything in nature is purposeful, whether we know the function or not. They keep looking for new organs that they can declare to be vestigial organs.

Stephen J. Gould was a leading evolutionist who wrote a book called *The Panda's Thumb*. He claimed that the panda's thumb was "poorly designed," a vestigial organ, and hence a proof for evolution. Today, studies have shown that the panda's thumb is perfectly designed for its function of grasping bamboo shoots and is "one of the most extraordinary manipulation systems" among mammals.

DINOSAURS

Whenever evolution is discussed, someone is bound to ask, "What about dinosaurs?" The general public has been conditioned by the evolutionist propaganda. They think that the once-upon-a-time existence of dinosaurs somehow demonstrates eons of time. They also believe that other species evolved from them, which the scientists do indeed claim (particularly birds). On what basis can they make this assumption? As mentioned earlier, it is the similarities in the body structure, homology and so-called transitional fossils.

These fossils actually prove nothing about any evolution ever having taken place. There certainly once were dinosaurs, and there are currently none in existence. They all died out, due to some unknown cause.[77] This is nothing unusual. Many species have become extinct in modern times,

---

76 Including on this author, who wants his tonsils back.

77 *Ma'aminim* can certainly postulate that the dinosaurs may have died in the *mabul*.

although nothing has evolved from those species. About one hundred and fifty years ago, there were billions of passenger pigeons, whose migration blocked out the sight of the sun even at mid-day. As far as we know, there are none left. They became extinct when they were over-hunted and their source of food or their habitat was destroyed. Nothing ever evolved from them. Extinction does not indicate evolution at all.

Dinosaur fossils were recently found in Montana with soft tissue containing blood cells. When Mary Schweitzer, of Montana State University's Museum of the Rockies, was examining a thin section of Tyrannosaurus Rex bone under her light microscope, she noticed a series of peculiar structures. Round and tiny and nucleated, they were threaded through the bone like red blood cells in blood vessels. But blood cells in a dinosaur bone should have disappeared eons ago. "I got goose bumps," recalls Schweitzer. "It was exactly like looking at a slice of modern bone. But, of course, I couldn't believe it. I said to the lab technician, 'The bones, after all, are sixty-five million years old. How could blood cells survive that long?' It's a very "good *kashya*," but it drives Schweitzer crazy when creationists suggest that this may be evidence for a recent creation. This is because she believes that geologists have established that the Hell Creek Formation, where the dinosaur bones were found, is sixty-eight million years old, and that therefore so are the bones buried in it. Remember that the theory, which states that all evolutionary changes came very gradually, requires eons of time. Were it correct that the dinosaurs are only a few thousand years old, it would constitute a threat not only to their estimation of the age of the earth, but to the entire theory as well.

PREHISTORIC MEN

As a boy, I often visited the Museum of Natural History in Manhattan. It is a museum dedicated to evolution. There they showed us pictures and statues of the prehistoric men from whom we supposedly evolved; the ancestors of modern men. It was very impressive. The more ancient, the more beast-like. It never entered my mind to doubt that this was all real and conclusive. However, the "prehistoric" men they depict in their museums and pictures are based on the finding of fossil parts that are totally open to interpretation. They have found thousands of fossils, and each one is recorded by number. For example, skull #1470, discovered in 1972 in Kenya, can be given a long face (if you push the upper jaw forward), or a short face (if you tuck it in). It all depends on how you hold it. National Geographic Magazine commissioned four artists to reconstruct the figure from fossils taken from the same species as skull #1470. One artist drew a creature that looked vaguely like a beaked dinosaur. Another artist drew a good-looking modern Afro-American with unusually long arms. Each depiction was totally different. With no other evidence available, it is impossible to reconstruct an authentic picture of the creature whose skull that was. It is just as possible to imagine on that skull the features of a modern professor as the features of an ape. These prehistoric men have been made to look as gruesome as possible. Some may have merely been a stooped ape or a person with arthritis. If you paint the pictures with a neat haircut, a suit and a tie they will look like nothing more than modern man. So they themselves have no way to know what that creature looked like when it was alive, but they have created in their picture books and museums an entire chain of creatures, from the most "prehistoric" until modern man. With absolutely nothing to base it on, this is a deception of the highest order. Their presentation of these findings is extremely biased.

EMBRYOLOGY

Embryology has been a mainstay of the theory from the time of Darwin on. The contention is twofold. First, that the embryos of mammals are all similar in their youngest stages, and this indicates that they all come from a common ancestor. They also claim that the embryo goes through a "recapitulation" of evolutionary stages. For example, they say that the human embryo has gill slits in the early stages of development, thus indicating that we once evolved from fish. The proof from embryology was considerably strengthened by the drawings of a German biologist name Ernst Haeckel, and Darwin considered embryology one of the strongest pieces of evidence for his theory. Haeckel's drawings were subsequently shown to be fraudulent. Human embryos never have gill slits, and an experienced eye can easily see the difference between one type of embryo and another even in their earliest stages.[78]

This so-called proof appeared in all textbooks, and was considered a major support for the theory. It still continues to appear in many textbooks, some even displaying the original fraudulent drawings of Haeckel.

AGE OF EARTH

The estimate of the age of the universe, the earth, and how long ago life appeared on earth are part and parcel of the theory of evolution. The entire theory would fall apart in the face of a young universe. As previously said, no macro-evolution has ever been observed taking place in the history of mankind. In order to justify the claim that evolution did indeed take place, they must say that even the slightest change happens so gradually that we haven't been around long enough to view it. Since evolution requires thousands of gradual changes to create a new organ or to get from one species to another, and each change takes very long, they must have billions of years at their disposal, or else the whole theory would fall apart. Hence, evolution and the age of the earth are a package deal. You can't have the one without the other.

How do they claim to know how old the earth is? Do they have a measuring tool the equivalent of a ruler, a thermometer or perhaps a Geiger counter[79] that enables them to measure time and gives them the exact date? There is nothing of the sort. They have a number of measuring methods, all based on various assumptions and enormous extrapolations, which are not borne out by the empirical evidence available.

The complex details of these measuring methods are not within the scope of this work. However, a synopsis is in order. Some elements decay over time, turning into a different element. For example, Uranium-238 (U238) will spontaneously decay over time until it transitions into Lead-206 (Pb206). Other elements decay in a similar fashion. By calculating the rate of decay during a short observable amount of time, measuring

---

[78] There is more to this fraud, but we will come back to it.

[79] These tools measure distance, temperature and radioactivity, respectively. There are no tools, however, to measure age.

the amount of Lead-206 in the rocks and extrapolating back millions or billions of years, scientists think they can know how old the rocks are.

There are a number of unproven assumptions on which this calculation is based. If any one of them were wrong, the whole measuring system would be invalid. First, the scientists assume that the rate of decay has been steady throughout the ages. If, in the unobservable past, the rate of decay was faster, then we have no way to determine the age of the rocks. Second, they assume that there was no Lead-206 in the rocks at the time of their formation. If there was, then we cannot determine how much decay has taken place since the formation of the rocks. There is a third consideration. If there are outside sources of contamination, then once again the rocks give us no clear indication of age.[80]

Other issues with the dating methods give us cause for skepticism. In an article that appeared in the bulletin of the Geological Society of America in January 2007, the following startling admission was made:

> Rocks in certain formations in South Africa which had previously been confidently declared to be 3.55 billion years old were now considered to be a mere 1.8 million years old.

What does this tell us about the reliability of the dating methods?[81]

In *Science Magazine*, 12 November 1999, page 1279, the following startling problem was recorded. In a certain rock formation in Italy, called

---

[80] According to our belief in *Torah*, the *mabul* could have produced enormous pressure which could have contaminated the rocks, giving them an appearance much older than they really are.

[81] Until the year 2007, the Barberton deposits in South Africa were confidently dated as among the most ancient geological formations on earth to a supposed age of 3.55 billion years (Archean) ... However, the latest evidence indicates that the supposedly ancient Barberton layers be promoted to the most recent geological layer of the Pleistocene epoch (putatively dated to have begun about 1.8 million years ago). Evolutionists regularly pointed to these rocks to make up stories about the origin of primitive life forms. Now we discover that these rocks "provide no information about conditions or life on the early Earth." The rocks could be forming today. Only evolutionists working in the Origin Sciences can be 99% wrong and still keep their jobs. Professionals such as Engineers and Doctors would not last too long with that kind of error rate. Engineers are also less likely to believe that chance and nature alone can explain the marvels of life than their evolutionary colleagues." *Bulletin of the Geological Society of America*, January 2007.

the Latemar, two different measuring methods yielded vastly different ages. One gave an age of eight million years old, and the second only two million years old. "Years of work on both ways of dating the Latemar have failed to resolve the conflict." One method must be faulty, but if one can be faulty then so can two.

Without going into the complex details, all authorities agree that carbon dating only works for things one hundred thousand years old or less. After that period, there will be no carbon-14 found because it will all have decayed. The scientist have long contended, based on their theories, that coal is millions of years old, and diamonds are billions of years old. However, carbon-14 has been found in both coal and diamonds. This indicates a severe fallacy in the dating methods.

THE COELACANTH FISH — ALIVE AND WELL

Students will seldom learn about the coelacanth fish. Based on the theorists' dating systems, the coelacanth fish was considered by evolutionists to have been extinct for sixty-five million years. Fossils in strata in which the coelacanth was found were also declared to be sixty-five million years old. All was well and good until subsequently this "extinct" fish was found swimming off the coast of Madagascar. A sixty-five million year error! What does this tell you about their dating system?

CHAPTER TWENTY-FIVE

Creation Is Not on Their Radar

The proponents of evolution offer many "proofs" that all living things descend from a common ancestor, and evolved through the eons into the myriad of species we see today. The proofs are often presented as conclusive evidence, an open and shut case, leaving no room for dissent, no option to suggest any other approach. If we review these proofs with a critical eye, unbiased by the aura of authority that most people attribute to the scientific community, we may see that this is hardly the case.

Let's go back for a moment to what our *emunah* teaches us. The six days of creation were the time when the Creator brought everything into existence via supernatural processes. Everything was created in a finished state. The first man (Adam haRishon) was a mature adult at the moment of his creation. The first chickens were fully developed at the moment they were created. Trees stood tall and fully grown. All species that would ever exist were already present from the beginning, and had no need to evolve. No intrinsically new creatures would ever come into being after the time of creation, although there has been some crossbreeding and many species have become extinct since then. This is what every observant Jew declares in the Friday night *Kiddush*. "The heavens and the earth and all their hosts were completed." The first Shabbos was the dividing line between the time of supernatural creation and the period when the world began to run according to the rules that the Creator put into nature, under His constant supervision. Infrequently performed miracles (such as the splitting of the Red Sea) are an exception to the rule, occurring only in very specialized circumstances.

When the scientists bring their proofs to substantiate their theory, they should be saying, "This works according to our thinking, but not according to yours. Hence it is a proof to us and a refutation of your belief." Generally, they just shoo us away with a wave of the hand, or condescendingly dismiss our position by saying that scientists subsequently demonstrated that creation cannot be correct. There are solid reasons for this behavior of theirs. In lots of cases, the evidence does not contradict creation, and for a person who subscribes to the *mesorah*, many of these proofs would fall by the wayside. For example, homologous creatures don't necessarily descend from a common ancestor. We say that they were designed by the Master Designer. These creatures all share some similar features with one another. Fossils they consider transitional were created with some features of one species and some of another, without having evolved from one into the other. Therefore, they don't want to even acknowledge creation as a serious option. If they did, they would be forced to admit that many of the proofs they offer are not incompatible with our *emunah* at all. So they simply present their proofs as conclusive and "game over."

There is a second reason as well, which complements the first. The evolutionists have an ironclad rule that serves as a defense mechanism. They call it methodological naturalism. This means that no explanation but a natural one is acceptable for the origins of the universe and all that is in it. Don't tell us about an intelligent designer, a Creator, or about G-d. Those are not scientific, natural explanations. So when they are asked if it is possible for a sensible human being to believe that the human brain evolved by gradual gene mutations, a direct response will not be forthcoming, because there can be no sensible response to this question. Rather, they will disqualify their opponents by saying that this line of reasoning is unscientific — it's against the rules.

Who made this rule? They did! The scientists themselves invented a rule that by definition does not allow for the possibility of intelligent design or creation to be discussed. If, however, your common sense tells you that the world could not have come about without an infinite intelligence behind it, then you also know that there is no validity to the rule of methodological naturalism.

ADMISSIONS

Some of the most renowned evolutionists have admitted openly that the main reason they cling to the theory (even though it has so many holes in it) is that they refuse to admit the possibility that there is a Creator.

Richard Dawkins, after describing the magnitude of the problem of the Cambrian explosion (according to two varying views of evolution), writes that both schools of evolutionists, "despise so-called scientific creationists equally, and both agree that the gaps are real, that there are true imperfections in the fossil record. Both schools of thought agree that the only alternative explanation of the sudden appearance of so many complex animal types in the Cambrian era is Divine creation, and both would reject this alternative." In plain English this means that we reject the idea of a Creator because we don't like it! However, the evidence is on the side of creation

Richard Lewontin, a top evolutionist, wrote the following admission:

> *Our willingness to accept scientific claims that are against common sense is the key to an understanding of the real struggle between science and the supernatural. We take the side of science in spite of the patent absurdity of some of its constructs, in spite of its failure to fulfill many of its extravagant promises of health and life, in spite of the tolerance of the scientific community for unsubstantiated just-so stories, because we have a prior commitment to materialism. It is not that the methods and institutions of science somehow compel us to accept a material explanation of the phenomenal world, but, on the contrary, that we are forced by our a priori adherence to material cause to create an apparatus of investigation and a set of concepts that produce material explanations, no matter how counterintuitive, no matter how mystifying to the uninitiated. Moreover,*

> that materialism is absolute, for we cannot allow a Divine foot in the door. The eminent Kant scholar Lewis Beck used to say that anyone who could believe in G-d could believe in anything. To appeal to an omnipotent deity is to allow that at any moment the regularities of nature may be ruptured, that miracles may happen.[82]

In this excerpt, Richard Lewontin has taught you that if you do believe in an omnipotent G-d, and that the regularities of nature are sometimes ruptured, and there is such a thing as miracles, then there is absolutely nothing compelling you to accept the theories. They have no proofs, only the desire to resist believing in a Creator.

One of the most famous paleontologists in the world, Harvard's Stephen Jay Gould, said, "The extreme rarity of transitional forms in the fossil record persists as the trade secret of paleontology."[83] This means that they know the fossil record proves nothing, but they are keeping it a secret.

WITHHOLDING INFORMATION

All the problems we have written about here are not secrets. They are discussed in the more sophisticated science books and journals. The critics of evolution have their say, and the scientists respond. Nevertheless, these problems are almost never presented to the general public, not in the media, nor in high school and university textbooks. They don't tell the public that dating methods contradict each other nor that fossilization in and of itself does not indicate antiquity. It isn't pointed out that microevolution does not equal macroevolution, and that sighting small changes within the existing species does not demonstrate the formation of new organs, and certainly not new species. Do the authors of biology textbooks not know that embryology has been discarded by many eminent authorities as any substantiation to evolution, and that Haeckel's drawings were shown long ago to be fraudulent? Shouldn't

---

82 Richard Lewontin, "Billions and Billions of Demons" (review of *The Demon-Haunted World: Science as a Candle in the Dark* by Carl Sagan, 1997), *The New York Review*, 9 January 1997, p. 31.

83 Stephen J. Gould, "Evolution's Erratic Pace," *Natural History*, vol. 86 (May 1987), p. 14.

the public know this? What about the lack of intermediate fossils and the glaring problem of the Cambrian explosion? Is that not something students should know about? Why is the establishment so vehemently opposed to the research of the proponents of intelligent design? Are they perhaps afraid that it will undermine the impression that the general public has, that all is well and good with the theory? What about the statements of eminent scientists, quoted earlier, who admit that their adherence to evolution is not based on evidence, but rather on their unwillingness to accept the belief in a Creator? All of this should certainly give a person pause when making a judgment as to the integrity of the evolutionist establishment.

AN ELEMENT OF DECEPTION

Not only are many vital issues concealed from the public, there are also numerous cases of open deception. Haeckel's drawings, long known to be fraudulent, still appear in textbooks. The peppered moth experiments are also an example of this. Peppered moths do not roost on tree trunks. The pictures were taken of moths that were put on the tree trunks manually. The exhibits of prehistoric men are very biased, and many of the so-called prehistoric fossils were proved to be fraudulent.

In light of all the above, let your common sense prevail. Could the human brain or the digestive system have come about through gene mutations? Did the coding in the DNA switch from one species to another by accident? Is there not endless intelligence and master design in everything we take the time to analyze? This is our intent here, to engage our *seichel* in this process, not to enter into the scientific debate with those who are wholly committed to the theory of evolution.

For those who need to go through that exercise, there are many excellent books on the subject, representing both sides. The reader is encouraged to do his research while bearing in mind the issues we have raised here. My intention here is merely to appeal to the reader's common sense, to realize that the theory of evolution is but a theory — and an unfounded one as well.

CHAPTER TWENTY-SIX

G-d-Guided Evolution?

Now we embark on a most distressing facet of our discussion. It is not only atheists who subscribe to this theory. There are people within the *frum* community who want to equate the belief in evolution with our *emunah*. Some of them are Orthodox scientists, who may be somewhat learned in Torah. Even some very reputable *talmidei chachamim* adopt or grant credibility to such a position. This position has been a source of great confusion in our communities. I consider it totally untenable. Hence, before we end this section, we need to address this position as well.

There can be various motives for sincere *frum* people supporting such an idea. Some find it discomforting to forsake the ideas that are popularly believed today in the secular world. They don't wish to be set apart, and therefore prefer to have the best of both worlds by accepting evolution, but somehow fitting it into the Torah scheme of things.[84]

Still others have a different motive, also sincere. They want to reach out to the secular community that has total faith in the scientific consensus,

---

84 Although suggesting a G-d-guided evolution already sets them far apart from the majority of scientists (who are atheists), they are still much more in line with them than if they discard evolution altogether.

and fear that if we tell them that in order to accept Torah they must abandon the currently accepted scientific consensus they will no longer be receptive to *kiruv* efforts.

Undoubtedly, all those mentioned above must simply feel that the evidence for evolution is overwhelming, based on the impressive array of research and proofs presented by the vast majority of the scientific community. They are confident that they are actually standing up for what they believe is the truth, all the while not sacrificing their adherence to Torah and *emunah*. Although their intention may be praiseworthy, their thinking is very flawed.[85]

FUNDAMENTAL QUESTIONS?

There are four basic questions that need to be asked before we proceed.

1. Is such a belief against the *mesorah*?
2. If it is, is there really any basis for abandoning a 3,300-year-old *mesorah*?
3. Even if the proofs were overwhelmingly solid, would we be allowed to alter the *mesorah*? (Perhaps we are obligated to stick with our *mesorah* no matter what, and have perfect faith that someday the "proofs" will be shown to be incorrect.)
4. Are we allowed to teach something that goes against the *mesorah* in order to be *mekarev Yidden*?

These questions are very fundamental and need to be addressed.

THE SIMPLE PSHAT

In order to accomplish this unique synthesis, scholars need to reinterpret entire segments of our Torah in ways that they were never understood before. Before we consider alternative explanations, let's look at the

---

85 There are other individuals who have very impure motives and actually intend to undermine the *mesorah*. We will not name them or address ourselves to them here. Others have already undertaken the task of responding to these people, and for us now that will have to suffice.

simple meaning of what the Torah tells us, and how it has always been understood by our people.

- The entire world was created in six days.
- Each day additional things were created. Each step was a new creation, not just an automatic natural result of the first day's creation.
- Trees were created on the third day, even before the sun and moon were yet placed in their orbits in the sky.[86]
- Adam was created on the sixth day. He was not born of parents, but rather created anew.
- On that same day, Chava was created.
- They were commanded by Hashem not to eat from the Tree of Knowledge.
- They transgressed the command and actually did eat on that same day. As a result, they were banished from Gan Eden.
- When Shabbos came, everything had been completed. Creation was over. Our observance of Shabbos commemorates the conclusion of all creation.

5775

The Torah gives us a chronology of the ten generations from Adam till Noach.

- In this chronology, we are told exactly how many years it was until each subsequent generation was born. One hundred thirty years till Shes, one hundred and five more years till Enosh, etc. The sum total tells us that Noach was born in the year 1056.
- In the end of *Parshas Noach* we have another chronology of the ten generations from Noach until Avraham.

---

86 The *Rishonim* speak extensively about how light and darkness could have existed and how time was measured before the sun and moon were hung in the sky. This discussion is not in the purview of this book.

- The bottom line of that calculation is that Avraham Avinu was born in the year 1948
- • Yitzchak Avinu was born one hundred years later, Yaakov Avinu sixty years after that.
- Although the Torah says that the Exodus from Egypt took place after four hundred years, *Chazal* prove to us from the verses that the *cheshbon* starts from the birth of Yitzchak, not from the time we entered Egypt.
- That brings us to the Exodus and the giving of the Torah in the year 2448.
- The verse in *Sefer Melachim* tells us that the Beis Hamikdash was built four hundred and forty years after *yetzias Mitzrayim*.
- The first Beis Hamikdash stood for four hundred and ten years, for a total of eight hundred and fifty years in the land. Now we are up to the year 3338.
- The Babyonian Exile lasted seventy years until they built the second Beis Hamikdash.
- The second Beis Hamikdash stood four hundred and twenty years. Secular history, as well as our records, has recorded that the Beis Hamikdash was destroyed in the year 68.[87] That was 1,947 years ago.[88] In our counting, that was 3828 from creation.
- This brings us to the calculation of 2015 in secular terms/5775 from creation.

All that we have just said is the surface meaning of the *Chumash*, Tanach and all subsequent historical records. Every *kesubah* is dated from creation. Ancient *sefarim* such as Rambam and Kuzari bring dates based on this calculation.

---

87 Note that there is some question as to exactly when it was destroyed, whether 68, 69 or 70 of the Common Era.

88 As of the time of this writing, 5775; 2015 in the common calendar.

SO FAR

So far we have learned that the Torah tells us that the world was created in six days. Adam and Chava were the first people, created directly by Hashem Yisborach Himself. They had no parents, and every human descends from them. Everything was completely finished by the first Shabbos, which was 5775 years ago. This is the simple meaning of the entire matter, and this is what our people have always believed.

A MAJOR REINTERPRETATION

Any attempt to equate our Torah with the theory of evolution will require a major reinterpretation of everything that we have just quoted, and a total refurbishment of the *emunah* of *Klal Yisrael*. In order to equate evolution with *emunah*, some Orthodox scientists postulate that the following new understandings must be introduced:

- The entire episode of *ma'asei Bereishis* must now be understood as nothing but a parable (*mashal*).
- Adam haRishon is merely a *mashal* for mankind as a whole.
- The stories of *Bereishis* are merely a *mashal* about the ultimate task of mankind
- Our version of history must also now include the whole story of evolution. This is how it goes: All living things evolved from a common one-celled ancestor over very long periods of time. This took hundreds of thousands, perhaps millions of years. G-d only made the original matter and the natural processes. He then supervised the evolutionary process, but was not directly involved. Rather, evolution happened through all natural processes. The supposed "six days of creation" are now to be understood as representing very long periods of time. Eventually the evolutionary processes brought about a race of hominids. These were apelike subhumans. Adam HaRishon was also born from a hominid mother and father. There wasn't only one such subhuman at the time, there was actually a whole race of them. However, then Hashem blew into these apelike creatures a *neshamah*, and that was the beginning of the human race.

A RED FLAG

When you hear this, doesn't this raise a red flag in your mind, as it does in mine? Even before we resort to the countless sources that contradict this, we have to ask ourselves a very obvious question. Is this some new kind of Judaism? Is this the belief that we inherited from our ancestors? Did anyone before our (very confused) generation ever understand *ma'asei Bereishis* in this manner? Did the prophets, the Men of the Great Assembly, the *Tannaim* or *Amoraim*? How about the more recent Sages, such as the *Vilna Gaon* or the *Chofetz Chaim*? Is the understanding of *ma'asei Bereishis* a scientific matter or a *mesorah* matter? Is there any other nation in the world that even claims to have a *mesorah* about the origins of the universe and life? To me, it is quite disturbing to realize that reputable people are ready to throw to the wind what they inherited from their predecessors.

WHAT DOES THE MESORAH SAY?

The entire Torah literature is full of statements in the clearest terms that the simple meaning of the Torah is what actually occurred. It is truly superfluous to even quote sources, because the entire Torah literature is full of this. The Gemara tells us that all species were originally created in full height and completed form. They didn't need to evolve. On the very first day, G-d created the length of day and night. The Gemara details for us what happened on the sixth day of creation, hour by hour, culminating in Adam haRishon coming to life, entering Gan Eden, sinning, and being banished from Gan Eden. All this took place before the first Shabbos. The Mishnah explains why humans were created with just one couple, in contrast to other species, which were created in multiples.

Here is the Sages' account of the sixth day of creation:

> מסכת סנהדרין דף לח עמוד ב
>
> אמר רבי יוחנן בר חנינא שתים עשרה שעות הוי היום שעה ראשונה הוצבר עפרו שניה נעשה גולם שלישית נמתחו אבריו רביעית נזרקה בו נשמה חמישית עמד על רגליו ששית קרא שמות שביעית נזדווגה לו חוה שמינית עלו למטה שנים וירדו ארבעה תשיעית נצטווה שלא לאכול מן האילן עשירית סרח אחת עשרה נידון שתים עשרה נטרד והלך לו

> *Rabbi Yochanan bar Chanina said, "The day is [divided into] twelve hours. The first hour his (Adam's) dust was collected, in the second he was made into a lifeless shape, in the third his limbs were stretched out, in the fourth a soul was thrown into him, in the fifth he stood up on his feet, in the sixth he called [all the creatures] names, in the seventh he was joined with Chava, in the eighth two went up to the bed and four came down, in the ninth he was commanded not to eat from the tree, in the tenth he sinned, in the eleventh he was judged, and in the twelfth he was banished and left [Gan Eden]."*

Concerning the length of day and night, this is what our *chachamim* had to say:

> מסכת חגיגה דף יב עמוד א
>
> ואמר רב יהודה אמר רב עשרה דברים נבראו ביום ראשון ואלו הן: שמים וארץ, תהו ובהו, אור וחשך, רוח ומים, מדת יום ומדת לילה.
>
> *Rav Yehuda said in the name of Rav, "Ten things were created on the first day and these are they: heaven and earth, tohu vavohu, light and darkness, wind and water, the measurement of day and the measurement of night."*

Rashi explains there that "the measurement of day and the measurement of night" means twenty-four hours.

Everything was created in a finished state:

> מסכת ראש השנה דף יא עמוד א
>
> דאמר רבי יהושע בן לוי כל מעשה בראשית בקומתן נבראו לדעתן נבראו לצביונן נבראו.
>
> *Rabbi Yehoshua ben Levi said, "All the works of Bereishis were created with their full height, with their assent, and in their unique form."*

There was no race of subhumans. The first couple was created alone.

> מסכת סנהדרין לז עמוד א
>
> לפיכך נברא אדם יחידי ללמדך שכל המאבד נפש אחת מישראל מעלה עליו הכתוב כאילו איבד עולם מלא וכל המקיים נפש אחת מישראל מעלה עליו הכתוב כאילו קיים עולם מלא.

G-d-Guided Evolution?

The following is what the *Rishonim* have to say about these matters. We quote only a little, but the unanimous consensus of our Sages is that the six days of creation were supernatural. The laws of nature came about with the arrival of Shabbos. The six days of creation were twenty-four hour days, and Adam haRishon was a real person, not a *mashal*.

> רמב"ם מורה נבוכים חלק שני אות ל
>
> וממה שצריך שתתבוננהו מאד זכרו בריאת אדם בששת ימי בראשית, אמר זכר ונקבה ברא אותם, וחתם הבריאה כלה ואמר, ויכלו השמים והארץ וכל צבאם, ופתח פתח אחד לבריאת חוה מאדם, וזכר עץ החיים ועץ הדעת ודבר הנחש והענין ההוא, וזכר שזה כולו היה אחר שהושם אדם בגן עדן, וכל החכמים מסכימים שזה העניין כלו היה ביום ששי, ושלא נשתנה עניין בשום פנים אחר ששת ימי בראשית, ולזה לא ירוחק דבר מן העניינים ההם כמו שאמרנו שעד הנה לא היה טבע נח.

> *From amongst the things that you must contemplate very much is that it [the Torah] mentions the creation of man in the six days of creation and it states: "He created them male and female." It concludes [the episode of] all of creation and states: "And the heavens and earth were completed and all of their hosts." After this it relates another beginning to the creation of [Adam and Chava and states that] Chava [came] from Adam, and it mentions the Tree of Life and Tree of Knowledge, and the story of the snake and what occurred, and it makes [i.e., establishes] that all this occurred after Adam was placed in Gan Eden. All of the wise men, may their memory be blessed, concur that this episode occurred on the sixth day [of creation] and that nothing will change after the six days of creation, and therefore none of the things from amongst those we mentioned [above] are distant [i.e., farfetched] because the laws of nature were not crystallized as of yet.*

> מהר"ל באר הגולה פרק ד
>
> דע, כי הוא יתברך הוציא את הנמצאים כולם לפעל המציאות בששת ימי בראשית בעצמו ובכבודו, לא על ידי שליח, הוא הטבע, כמו שהיה אחר ששת ימי בראשית, שהשם יתברך מנהיג עולמו על ידי השליח, והוא הטבע.

> *Know that He, may His name be blessed, caused all of reality to materialize into existence during the six days of creation Himself, in His own glory, and not through the agency of nature, as opposed to the period which ensues*

after the six days of creation in which Hashem, may His name be blessed, governs his creation via the intermediary of nature. (Maharal[89])

The first man was no allegory at all, but rather a real person.

רמב״ם הלכות בית הבחירה פרק ב הלכה א-ב

המזבח מקומו מכוון ביותר ואין משנין אותו ממקומו לעולם שנאמר זה מזבח לעולה לישראל. ובמקדש נעקד יצחק אבינו שנאמר ולך לך אל ארץ המוריה ונאמר בדברי הימים ויחל שלמה לבנות את בית ד' בירושלים בהר המוריה אשר נראה לדוד אביהו אשר הכין במקום דוד בגרן ארנן היבוסי. ומסורת ביד הכל שהמקום שבנה בו דוד ושלמה המזבח בגורן ארונה הוא המקום שבנה בו אברהם המזבח ועקד עליו יצחק והוא המקום שבנה בו נח כשיצא מן התיבה והוא המזבח שהקריב עליו קין והבל ובו הקריב אדם הראשון קרבן כשנברא ומשם נברא. אמרו חכמים אדם ממקום כפרתו נברא.

The geographical location of the mizbe'ach was extremely precise; its location is never to be altered… It is a tradition in the hands of all that the place Dovid and Shlomo built the mizbe'ach in Goren Aravnah, in the same place that Avraham built the mizbe'ach to which he tied Yitzchak. It is the place which Noach built upon when he exited the ark. It is the mizbe'ach which Kayin and Hevel offered upon and Adam haRishon sacrificed a korban when he was created. And from there he was created. Our Sages have said, "Adam was born from the dust located at the place of his atonement."[90]

From all the above we see without a doubt what the position of the *mesorah* is.

AFTER ASKING FORGIVENESS

I give the people who espouse these ideas the benefit of the doubt. Undoubtedly, they are intimidated by the array of scientists, the proofs and the rest of the propaganda. I assume they have not researched the matter thoroughly enough to realize that there is absolutely no reason to be intimidated.

However, with all due respect to the people who say this, it is not

---

89   Be'er haGolah 4, p. 83.

90   Hilchos Beis haBechira 2:1–2.

necessary to give credibility to anyone in this matter. No one has a right to tamper with our *mesorah*, even a great *talmid chachom*. The *mesorah* is not *hefker*. I cannot, in my wildest imagination envision the Chofetz Chaim, *zt"l*, agreeing to change the understanding of the *mesorah* in order to accommodate the theories of Darwin and the Neo-Darwinists. If the *Chofetz Chaim* were still alive today, would one of these reputable scholars be able to look him straight in the eye and tell him this new version of *emunah*? I think they would be too embarrassed to face him.[91] We may (perhaps) forgive them for their error, and appreciate their good intentions, but we cannot accept that which corrupts our *mesorah*.

FOR WHAT REASON?

There is, however, another crucial consideration. We have already shown that the theory of evolution is nothing less than incredible. It flies in the face of plain common sense. The proofs are not proofs. Two plus two does not equal five. Every proof has dissenters, even amongst the scientists who do subscribe to evolution. There are even a significant amount of credible scientists who do not subscribe to the theory at all. The media propaganda is very biased and one sided. On what basis should anyone even consider relinquishing the beliefs of *Am Yisoel*, by which we have lived and for which we have so often died?

When the theory of evolution first came out, many of our scholars were intimidated by it. They may have felt they had no choice but to try somehow to accommodate it by "fitting it in." By now, however, there is enough material to refute it and its proofs that no one need feel any pressure to fit it into our *mesorah*.

---

91 Even with interpretations which may (or may not) "fit" into the *pesukim*.

CHAPTER TWENTY-SEVEN

How Can People Be Oblivious to the Obvious Truth?

To start with, most people simply don't think through things carefully. They follow whatever the current popular belief is, assuming that everything has been checked out, and that all has been proved precisely as they have been told. The masses read the newspapers and other media and follow blindly. Many of the scientists fall into this category as well. They, too, were taught the theory of evolution since their youth. Most of them have never done the experiments or measurements themselves.

The scientists in the forefront of the evolutionary debates know everything we have written here. There is no dispute about the marvels and complexities of what they call "nature." They surely know how many systems are required to participate in eating an apple, bringing its nourishment to the body and eliminating the wastes. They also are well-aware of the astounding complexity of the human brain. How can they deny the existence of a Creator and claim that all this came about by a series of lucky accidents that just happened to complement each other?

There is a good reason why the most knowledgeable don't recognize the Creator. Pay careful attention to the answer, because it is very important.

WHEN YOU START WITH AN AGENDA

If the atheists have made up their minds that they don't want to accept the idea of a G-d, nothing will change their minds. Their answers may be so farfetched as to border on the ridiculous,[92] but that won't deter them. No matter what it takes, they will not admit the truth. As quoted above, many scientists have stated openly that they adhere to the theory because they will not allow themselves to admit that there is a Creator.[93]

Is it really possible for any sensible (unbiased, objective) person to think that all natural things came about by what amounts to a series of lucky accidents? Can the miracles of childbirth or the respiratory system have evolved gradually by errors in the genes? As we said earlier, even before you examine the evidence, you know that their "proofs" must be flawed, because evolution goes against common sense, and hence is simply incredible.

Reb Elchonon Wasserman wrote an essay about *emunah* (quoted earlier), wherein he asks many questions: How can the Torah obligate every Bar Mitzvah boy or Bas Mitzvah girl to believe in Hashem, when even the greatest of philosophers did not come to believe in Him? Why is it that the Torah refers to thoughts of heresy (disbelief) as "straying after the heart?" Isn't disbelief an issue of the mind rather than the heart?

He answers that a person need not be a philosopher to come to the belief

---

92 The winners of the Nobel Prize for discovering DNA came to realize the flaws in the traditional evolutionary argument. They came up with an alternative theory called "panspermia." This theory states "that life on Earth was seeded from space, and that life's evolution to higher forms depends on genetic programs that come from space." Of course, this just moves the problem a little further away. There still needed to be a designer somewhere. Another eminent scientist said that there is nothing to worry about. Only the outer space creatures owe Him allegiance, not we.

93 It is absolutely true that the scientists will respond by saying that we are the ones who have the agenda. We want to grasp the straw of belief in a Creator, and therefore we reject their theories. Such a position might have made sense before we went through all their proofs, and showed how they don't add up. At this point, their position makes no sense, ours does. We can state with certainty that they are the ones who have the agenda, not we. All the more so, when some of their most eminent authorities have stated so explicitly.

in the Ribono shel Olam, because nothing could be more obvious than the existence of an infinitely intelligent Creator. It is the contrary that is astonishing. How could the brilliant philosophers (such as Aristotle) not believe? It makes no sense at all!

Our Torah reveals all hidden matters to us, and has shed light on this question as well. A judge is forbidden to accept a bribe or even a present from one of the litigants. Not only if he is asked to favor the litigant who gives the present, but even if no demands or requests are made of him, he still can't accept a bribe. The Torah says, "Because a bribe blinds the eyes of the wise and distorts the words of the righteous." No matter how objective the judge may try to be, his mind has been biased because of that gift.

So, too, in the matter of belief, says Reb Elchonon. If a person is driven by his desire to be free from restrictions, he becomes blinded to even the most obvious realities.

Reb Elchonon continues:

> קובץ מאמרים מר' אלחנן וסרמן זצ"ל (מאמר הראשון: מאמר על האמונה)
> היוצא מזה כי יסודי האמונה מצד עצמם הם פשוטים ומוכרחים לכל אדם שאיננו בכלל שוטה, אשר אי אפשר להסתפק באמיתתם. אמנם רק בתנאי שלא יהא האדם משוחד, היינו שיהא חפשי מתאות עולם הזה ומרצונותיו. ואם כן סיבת המינות והכפירה אין מקורה בקלקול השכל מצד עצמו כי אם מפני רצונו לתאוותיו, המטה ומעור את שכלו ומעתה מובן היטב מה שהזהירה תורה "ולא תתורו אחרי לבבכם" "זו מינות" היינו שהאדם מוזהר להכניע ולשעבד את רצונותיו.

What comes out of this is that the fundamentals of emunah themselves are simple and unavoidable to any person that is not in the category of the insane. It is impossible to doubt their truth. However, this is only on condition that the person is free from the longing for this world and from his own desires. If so, the cause of heresy and denial does not have its source in the distortion of the intellect itself, but rather because of the person's desire for his lusts. This distorts and blinds his intellect. Now it can be very well understood why the Torah commands, "Do not stray after your heart" (which refers to heresy). That means that a person is commanded to humble and subjugate his desires (so that he can remain objective to see the obvious truth).

So, some people (including some scientists) are swept along by the propaganda, and have not analyzed the issues objectively. They are similar to Larry in the story told above. However, by their own admission, there are eminent scientists who don't see what any other sensible person can see, simply because they don't want to see it. Admitting Divine design would change their lives — and they don't want their lives changed. Although it is indeed true that the mind is the source of our thoughts, the heart (which is the source of our emotions and our desires) influences the mind. When a person has an agenda to resist the discipline of the Creator, they will believe only what fits their agenda and allows them the freedom to do whatever they please. Hence, the Torah attributes heresy to the heart more than to the mind.

WHEN WE LIVE BY THE EMUNAH

Actually, we shouldn't be fazed by the propaganda of the evolutionists. *Klal Yisrael* has had to withstand competing philosophies ever since the inception of our nation.

- The idol worshippers thought we were crazy to worship a G-d whom we cannot see. They outnumbered us many, many times over. We didn't care. We knew our *emunah* was true and we stuck by it.

- Throughout the years in Christian Europe we were viewed as outcasts because we didn't accept their beliefs. They put us in ghettos, made discriminative laws against us, and limited our opportunities for earning a living and leading a normal life.

- The missionaries have harassed us with their "Bible proofs" all through the centuries. But we know that we received a Torah directly from Hashem Yisborach on Har Sinai. We know we have a *mesorah* back to the very first day when He spoke to us personally. We are absolutely confident that our forefathers didn't lie to us when they gave this *mesorah* over to us. So they can bring us as many proofs as they want, we still won't budge an inch away from the *emunah*. We will wait patiently until their proofs are refuted and their theories discarded.

It is exactly the same with evolution. We know that "In the beginning Hashem created heaven and earth." Nothing can shake us from that belief. Even if all their proofs would be utterly convincing and totally conclusive, we would assume that they are flawed and that someday soon we will be able to see the flaws in them.

How much more so is this true when every proof has eminent scientists that reject it; when the fossil record itself refutes all their claims, when we know that they have no empirical evidence whatsoever? The entire universe demonstrates the wisdom of the Master Creator. Their claims won't even make a dent in our three-thousand-year-old *emunah* in Hashem and in His Torah.

IN CONCLUSION

Besides the shallowness of all the so-called proofs, common sense dictates that the world had to be designed by an infinite intelligence. Isn't it self-evident that the human brain, respiratory system, circulatory system and digestive system were designed with the utmost precision to fulfill their very complex functions to perfection? A healthy body has millions of machines all working in harmony. The scientist who can convince me that my heart or brain is the result of endless lucky accidents has not yet been born!

The existence of the Creator is evident wherever we turn. For the sake of brevity, only a detail or two was given about each of the fascinating testimonies we have cited. In the scope of this essay, it isn't possible to even scratch the surface. Now that your attention has been drawn to this, you can continue observing, reading and strengthening your *emunah* in the *Borei Olam* all your life. You can be one hundred percent confident that (as we learned from *Sefer Hachinuch*) it is simply impossible any other way, and the theories of the evolutionists will not affect your conviction one iota.

CHAPTER TWENTY-EIGHT

Please Don't Take My Word For It

Now that we have come to the end of our discussion about evolution, I have to add one more thought. That is, please don't take my word for it. I am not an authority, and don't expect anyone to rely on my writings to make their judgment. Whoever feels that they need to investigate further and give the evolutionists their chance to answer, is more than welcome to do so. However, it is important for you to know that almost nothing that has been written in this section is my original thinking. These problems are very real, and they are no secret to anyone who delves beyond the simplistic version that has been presented to the public. I highly doubt that the reader will find any more satisfaction with the scientists' response than I have. My purpose here was to make the issues known to all, so that everyone should realize that the matter is not nearly as it has been presented. This is true for everyone, but especially for someone true to our *emunah*. Our *mesorah* is eternal, has withstood all the philosophies of old, and will continue to survive long after the theory and all its works will have been discarded on the junk heap of history.

SUMMING UP

I hope that the reader has begun to see with his/her own *seichel* that the *mesorah* we received from our forebearers is no made-up story, fairy tale or folklore. Rather, it is indeed incontrovertible. We have only begun our climb from the most basic basement level of *emunah* to the higher floors. Let me share with you just one more vital piece about what awaits you when you get to the top.

CHAPTER TWENTY-NINE

The Emunah Sugar Cube

When your *emunah* is clear and strong, and you know without a shadow of a doubt that the Torah is from the Ribono shel Olam, then you will also know that He Himself has told us that everything in His Torah was given to us only for our good. A human being is not merely composed of a body. He is a combination of a *guf* and a *neshamah*. Only our Torah teaches us how to be fulfilled and satisfied, both in body and soul. This is what we learn clearly in the *Chumash*.

> דברים פרק י׳ פסוק יב-יז
>
> ועתה ישראל מה ד' אלקיך שאל מעמך כי אם ליראה את ד' אלקיך ללכת בכל דרכיו ולאהבה אתו ולעבד את ד' אלקיך בכל לבבך ובכל נפשך: לשמר את מצות ד' ואת חקתיו אשר אנכי מצוך היום לטוב לך: הן לד' אלקיך השמים ושמי השמים הארץ וכל אשר בה: רק באבתיך חשק ד' לאהבה אותם ויבחר בזרעם אחריהם בכם מכל העמים כיום הזה:
>
> *And now, Yisrael, what does Hashem, your G-d ask of you? Only to fear Hashem, your G-d, to go in all His ways and to love Him, to serve Hashem, your G-d with all your heart and all your life. To guard the mitzvos of Hashem and His statutes which I command you today, for your good. Behold! Hashem, your G-d owns the heavens and the heavens above the heavens, the earth and all that is in it. Only in your forefathers did Hashem*

> *delight to love them. He chose their descendants after them (that is you), like this very day.*

It couldn't be any clearer than this. The Creator of the Universe is telling us that the entire Torah system has been given to us solely for our good. Perhaps we don't appreciate this sufficiently, especially when we are young. Nevertheless, it is absolutely true. This idea is expressed very beautifully in the *Sefer Hachinuch*.

> ספר החינוך מצוה צה באמצע הדברים
>
> דע בני כי כל אשר יגיע אצל השם בעשות בני אדם מצותיו איננו רק שחפץ השם להטיב לנו. ובהיות האדם מוכשר ומוכן בעשיית אותן מצות לקבל הטובה אז ייטיב אליו ד' ועל כן הודיעם דרך טוב להיותם טובים והיא דרך התורה. ... ופרשה אחת נכתבה בתורה להודיענו עיקר זה והוא מה שכתוב 'ועתה ישראל וכו' לטוב לך'. כלומר איננו שואל מעמך דבר בעשותך מצותיו רק שרצה בטובו הגדול להטיב לך וכמו שכתוב אחריו 'הן לד' אלקיך השמים ושמי השמים הארץ וכל אשר בה' כלומר ואינו צריך למצותיך רק מאהבתו אותך לזכותך.
>
> *Know, my son, that the only thing that Hashem derives from people doing His mitzvos is that He wants to do good for us. When a person is prepared and ready, through doing the mitzvos, to receive the good, then Hashem will grant him that good. Therefore, He informed them of the good path, (the way of the Torah), so that they can become good people... A special parshah has been written in the Torah to inform us of this fundamental idea. That is what is written, "Now, Yisrael, what does Hashem want from you, etc., only for your good." This means that Hashem asks nothing of you in your doing His mitzvos other than that He wants, in His great goodness, to do good to you. As is written after this, "Behold! Hashem, your G-d owns the heavens and the heavens above the heavens, the earth and all that is in it. Only in your forefathers did Hashem delight to love them. He chose their descendants after them (that is you), like this very day." This means that He does not need your mitzvos, but only out of His love for you to give you merit.*

The very idea that a life of Torah deprives a person of the joys of life is a fallacy. A person who is a *ma'amin* is able to enjoy life and partake of the good things of this world just as much as the person who is not a *ma'amin*.

He can eat his full of the finest foods, wear well-tailored, attractive clothing and sleep in a comfortable bed. He can run a successful business, become a professional or engage in a craft. He can choose who to marry, enjoy a normal married life and raise a beautiful family.

True, shrimp and pork are forbidden. Instant gratification is not always permissible. However, a prerequisite for happiness (even for secular people) is learning to live with self-control. Without self-control, people over-indulge and do themselves great harm. Torah restrictions teach us this self-control, without forbidding anything that would put a damper on life. We are advised not to over-indulge, and not to make physical pleasures an end to themselves. Rather, we use the physical to fuel our bodies and enable us to pursue the spiritual. Hence, the *ben Torah* can enjoy the physical world, while utilizing the self-control that the Torah teaches us. This will enable him to accomplish his mission in life, in the knowledge that when this ends something even better awaits him.

We hope to write, *b'ezras Hashem*, more about this subject. For now, however, we will just store away in our minds the idea that the entire Torah was given to us for our good, and that the *ma'amin* can actually enjoy life much more than someone who does not believe.

IN CONCLUSION

Many other issues still remain to be written about and clarified. We need to show that the *Torah She-ba'al Peh* is the *d'var Hashem*, that the ways of *hashgachah* are (at least somewhat) understandable even to our simple minds, that true *simchas ha-chaim* is to be found only by going in the *derech Hashem*, and much more. In the meanwhile, keep thinking about the thoughts presented here. Let them continue circulating in your mind, until you get a solid grip on the *emunah* by which your people have lived, and for which they have died, for over three thousand years.

אמן!

About the Author

Rabbi Dovid Sapirman is a former *talmid* of the Philadelphia, Ponivez, and Lakewood Yeshivos. During his forty-three years in the field of *chinuch*, he has been a *melamed, magid shiur, mashgiach ruchani*, public speaker, and worked extensively in *kiruv rechokim* and *kiruv k'rovim*.

With nearly four decades of experience focusing on reinforcing core *emunah*, he founded the Ani Ma'amin Foundation in 2009. It is dedicated to offering *chizuk* in *emunah* to Bnei Torah of all ages and backgrounds. In only a few years, the foundation has held presentations for over forty thousand people around the world, and created three popular series of CDs on *inyanei emunah*. Rabbi Sapirman lives in Toronto, Canada, with his family.

About Mosaica Press

Mosaica Press is an independent publisher of Jewish books. Our authors include some of the most profound, interesting, and entertaining thinkers and writers in the Jewish community today. There is a great demand for high-quality Jewish works dealing with issues of the day — and Mosaica Press is helping fill that need. Our books are available around the world. Please visit us at www.mosaicapress.com or contact us at info@mosaicapress.com. We will be glad to hear from you.

MOSAICA PRESS

לעילוי נשמת
ר' ישראל בן נפתלי הנדלסמן ע"ה
עבר שנות השואה ונשאר עובד ד' בתמימות כל ימיו

נדבת בנו ומשפחתו

לעילוי נשמת ר' עקיבא איגר בן חיים יחזקאל ע"ה

לעילוי נשמת בלימא שבע עלקא בת ר' גרשון ע"ה

לעילוי נשמת שרה בת צביה ע"ה

לעילוי נשמת שמואל יעקב בן שמעון ע"ה

לעילוי נשמת ישראל בן פייול ע"ה

לעילוי נשמת
הינדא בת ר' שמואל ברוך הלוי
אשת האי גברא רבא ר' אלימלך טרעס ע"ה

לעילוי נשמת אברהם בן שאול ע"ה

לעילוי נשמת גרשום בן אשר ע"ה
שרה בת ישי ע"ה
סלאמון בן אבולגיה ע"ה

לעלוי נשמת האשה החשובה חיה שרה בת ר' אהרן ע"ה

לעלוי נשמת שמואל יעקב בן יצחק אייזק משולם ע"ה

לעלוי נשמת רחל לאה בת שמואל ע"ה

לעלוי נשמת שלמה אהרן בן צבי הלל ע"ה

לעלוי נשמת שיינדל בת יחזקאל פייול ע"ה

יעקב מנחם מנדל בן מאיר ע"ה

חיה בת יחזקאל ע"ה

פנחס בן יואל ע"ה

משה צבי בן אברהם יצחק ע"ה

איתה בת דוב בערל ע"ה

צבי משה דיימן ע"ה

חנה דיימן ע"ה

לעלוי נשמת הענא בת אלחנן ע"ה

לעלוי נשמת חיים בן אברהם ע"ה

מלכה בת אהרן ע"ה

מיכאל בן שמואל שמעון ע"ה

רחל בת מאיר ע"ה

לעלוי נשמת שולמית בת מרדכי ניסן ע"ה

לעלוי נשמת אריה לייב בן אברהם ע"ה

לעלוי נשמת הרב יקותיאל בן יוסף ע"ה
צפורה בת החבר אברהם יוסף שמחה הכהן ע"ה

לעלוי נשמת יצחק יואל בן מנחם נחום הכהן ע"ה
נדבת מנחם ושרה לאה קובקס

לעלוי נשמת ירחמיאל בן יהודה לייב הלוי ע"ה

נדבת דניאל ומיכל בלזם לע"נ פינחס בן יצחק בלזם ע"ה

לעלוי נשמת יעקב מאיר בן משה ע"ה

לעלוי נשמת ר' זאב בן ר' יצחק מאיר ע"ה
לעלוי נשמת חנה בת ר' אברהם אבא ע"ה